Poles Apart?

Eastern European attitudes to healthcare reform

The Stockholm Network

The Stockholm Network is a one-stop shop for organisations seeking to work with Europe's brightest policy-makers and thinkers. Our unique network of over 130 market-oriented think tanks in Europe and farther afield provides unparalleled access to the best European policy thinking, the opportunity to lead debates, to change the climate of ideas in Europe, and to meet the key players in shaping the policy debates of tomorrow.

Poles Apart?

Eastern European attitudes to healthcare reform

Helen Disney, David Hill, Pavel Hrobon, Adam Kruszewski,
Henrieta Madarová, Rick Nye, Martin Stefunko

STOCKHOLM NETWORK

Populus

First published in Great Britain in 2005 by
The Stockholm Network
35 Britannia Row
London N1 8QH
www.stockholm-network.org

in association with Profile Books Ltd

The Stockholm Network is Europe's only dedicated service organisation for market-oriented think tanks and thinkers

A CIP catalogue record for this book is available from the British Library.

ISBN 0 9547663 3 4

Designed by Sue Lamble
Typeset in Stone Serif by MacGuru Ltd
info@macguru.org.uk

Printed and bound in Great Britain by Hobbs the Printers

Contents

About the authors

Helen Disney is Director of the Stockholm Network, a service organisation for Europe's market-oriented think tanks and thinkers. She was formerly a leader writer and commentator for *The Times* and the *Daily Express*, and continues to contribute regularly to the print and broadcast media. Before entering journalism, she was Deputy Director of the Social Market Foundation, an independent think tank, and editor of its quarterly journal. She is the editor of a number of think tank publications including *The Sex Change Society* (by Melanie Phillips), *Europe's Welfare Burden, Breaking Down the Barriers, Impatient for Change, An Apology for Capitalism* and *A Sick Business – counterfeit medicines and organised crime.*

David Hill has lived in central and eastern Europe for more than a decade, working mainly in journalism. This has included periods as editor-in-chief of the *Budapest Business Journal* (both English and Hungarian language editions), being one of the founding team of *Bucharest Business Week*, and stringing for The *Economist* Group and the financial newswire Mergermarket, as well as guest-editing the blog Pestiside.hu. He is also a writer and translator of poetry and lyrics. He has a degree in German and Russian from Oxford University, and is also proficient in Romanian and Hungarian. His website is www.davidhill.biz

Pavel Hrobon is a medical doctor and an adviser to the CEO of the General Health Insurance Fund (VZP) of the Czech Republic. He is also a founding member of the non-governmental initiative Health reform.cz, whose aim is to prepare a complex proposal for reforming the Czech healthcare system. Dr Hrobon has an MD from Charles University in Prague and a Master of Science degree in health policy and management from the Harvard School of Public Health. Between 1998 and 2002, he worked as a consultant for McKinsey & Company in Prague, where he has consulted for clients on healthcare, insurance and banking issues in several European countries.

Adam Kruszewski is a former physician turned healthcare entrepreneur who has helped to start up a number of healthcare-related businesses in central and eastern Europe. More recently he has been working as a consultant to the Polish Minister of Economy on the Polish health reform proposals. Since 1996, he has also given lectures on healthcare management for the School of Public Health, Project Hope and others. In 2003 and 2004, he was nominated in the medical press as one of the 100 most influential people in the Polish healthcare sector.

Henrieta Madarová is a co-founder and member of the Health Policy Institute. From 2002 to 2005 she was a member of the healthcare reform team of Rudolf Zajac, Minister of Health of Slovakia.

Rick Nye is a Director of Populus, whose opinion-polling clients include *The Times* and a range of private companies and public institutions. He served as Director of the Conservative Research Department from 1999 to 2003, speechwriting for successive Conservative leaders and co-ordinating the Party's polling and advertising campaigns during the 2001 General Election. Previously he was Director of the Social Market Foundation, a think tank dedicated to reforming welfare and injecting greater personal accountability into Britain's healthcare and education systems. A frequent contributor to newspapers and commentator on TV and radio, his publications include *The Future of Welfare* (ed.), *Welfare to Work* and *Panacea or Placebo*, examining public attitudes to private involvement in the NHS.

Martin Stefunko is co-founder of the Slovak free market think tank, the Institute for Free Society, based in Bratislava. He holds a PhD in Economic Theory and the History of Economic Thought from the Economic University of Bratislava, Slovakia, and is a visiting fellow of the Centre for the New Europe, a pan-European think tank, based in Brussels. He was a research fellow with the Mises Institute, Auburn, USA, in 2000–2001 and is the author of more than a hundred articles in newspapers and scientific journals.

Glossary

Our survey defines patients' views using a variety of criteria, derived from cross-tabulation of the poll findings. The key terms used in this introduction and in the country reports which follow are defined as follows:

Delivery Deficit

Populus identified five key factors associated with good quality health systems and asked respondents to rate whether these factors were important to them in their health system. They were then asked how well they felt their own system delivered them. The total number of responses indicating that a system was good at delivering a particular feature, such as access to new medicines and technology, for example, was deducted from the proportions who felt that feature of healthcare to be important. An average Delivery Deficit for each country was derived from the mean score of each feature.

Solidarity Gap

This figure is the difference between those who believe equality of access to the same standards of healthcare is more important than the quality of care experienced by the individual.

Inferiority Complex

The Inferiority Complex is designed to measure how respondents view their system in comparison with those of other nations. People were asked for an opinion on whether their own system performed better, worse or about the same as those of other European countries. For those who expressed a view, the scores for those responding 'the same' or 'worse' were deducted from the score for 'better' to produce an overall Inferiority Complex rating for each country.

Pessimism Ranking

The Pessimism Ranking examines the prospects for health systems in the future if no reform takes place in the next decade. The total of those who believe things will improve is deducted from the total of those who think the situation will remain the same or deteriorate.

Reform Index

We asked respondents to assess whether their health systems needed reform and, if so, how urgently. We then ranked countries on a Reform Index by deducting the percentage who felt reform was unnecessary from those who felt reform was desirable or urgent.

Acknowledgements

A number of friends and colleagues gave up their time and intellectual firepower to make this book a reality. In particular, many thanks to all the authors from central and eastern Europe for their insights and for turning around their chapters and page proofs to a very tight deadline. As ever, Rick Nye and colleagues at Populus compiled the data and graphs beautifully and made the job of analysing them a very straightforward one. Profile Books took the raw material and turned it into a coherent finished product with their usual aplomb. Within the Stockholm Network office, Terry O'Dwyer took firm charge of launching the book and liaising with our affiliates from Warsaw to Bratislava. Last and certainly not least, we extend our gratitude to our local partner think tanks, without whom the book would never be able to reach and influence such a large audience. We hope the ideas and opinions it contains continue to travel far and wide.

part 1

Introduction

Introduction

Helen Disney and Pavel Hrobon

What do the European public think about their healthcare systems now and what do they expect from them in the future? How will the increasing demand for healthcare, common to all modern democracies, be paid for and managed as time goes on and as the public become active consumers rather than passive patients?

In 2004, the Stockholm Network commissioned Populus to conduct a survey of eight European Union countries in order to find out the answers to these and other questions. The results were published in book form under the title *Impatient for Change: European attitudes to healthcare reform*.

We felt, however, that it was not enough to look just at the situation in the original fifteen EU member states. Just over a year ago, on 1 May 2004, the Union expanded to encompass ten new member states, mostly from the former communist nations of central and eastern Europe. How did attitudes there compare with those in the west, and was there anything to be learned from their differing approaches to reform?

In this volume, therefore, new poll findings from Slovakia, Hungary and Poland, conducted in early 2005, have been added to the original findings published in the *Impatient for Change* study. The overall data published in *Poles Apart?* has thus been expanded to include eleven EU member states in total, of which four are new member states.

Analysing 2005's results alongside those for 2004, we are able to begin to offer a comparison between the views of those people living in established EU countries and those of people in nations who have recently joined the Union.

We have included the 2004 results for the Czech Republic alongside this year's responses from Slovakia, Hungary and Poland to generate figures for the four new member states (NMS4) and set these alongside the EU7 (Britain, France, Germany, Italy, the Netherlands, Spain and Sweden).

Poles apart?

It is often assumed that the new member states and the rest of the EU states must be poles apart, not just geographically, but also when it comes to the state of their healthcare systems and their voters' attitudes towards them.

Slovakia, Poland and Hungary all emerged from the yoke of communism with state-run, state-funded systems that were highly bureaucratic, mismanaged and often corrupt. For many citizens, the only way they could get access to health-care treatment was to offer under-the-counter cash bribes to their physicians – and some still do today. Systems were also largely under-funded, especially in comparison with other EU nations.

However, since the fall of communism, all three countries have undertaken healthcare reforms to a greater or less extent. Slovakia, in particular, has been at the forefront of pushing for a more market-oriented approach to healthcare and a more consumer-driven system. This urgency has been created in part because of the economic strictures imposed by European Union membership and partly because of demand from their citizens for better services and a better standard of living. Below we take a look at how these systems have operated in the past and what has happened since, before going on to examine the poll findings and what they tell us about the prospects for reform in both the east and the west.

Eastern European healthcare systems – how do they work?

The new EU member states from central and eastern Europe covered in this report (Czech Republic, Hungary, Poland and Slovakia) seem to be a rather compact group measured by history and GDP per capita. Patients and physicians in these countries are historically used to living with the communist model of highly centralised national health systems, where many new treatments and medicines, and even some old ones, were rationed.

All of them have also initiated fairly substantial healthcare reforms in the last decade of the twentieth century, since the Berlin Wall fell. However, a closer look reveals significant differences in funding, organisation and recent developments in their respective healthcare systems. This suggests that it would be a mistake to treat them as a single bloc, just as it is impossible to talk about other European systems en masse, since their history, funding systems and types of provision vary so widely.

Table 1 **Total expenditure on health funding as proportion of GDP**

	2002
Czech Republic	7.4
France	9.7
Germany	10.9
Hungary	7.8
Italy	8.5
Netherlands	9.1
Poland	6.1
Slovakia	5.7
Spain	7.6
Sweden	9.2
United Kingdom	7.7

(Source: OECD Health Data 2004, 3rd edition)

On the funding side, the Czech Republic and Hungary spend almost 60% more per capita than Poland or Slovakia, measured by purchasing power parity. These relatively high levels of spending are, nevertheless, significantly lower than in the majority of the 'old' EU member states. The share of public expenditure devoted to health ranges from 70% in Hungary to over 90% in the Czech Republic.

Despite these differences, all of the new member states currently face a significant deficit in healthcare financing. The Czechs and Slovaks rely on multiple competing payers, while the Poles and Hungarians finance their providers through a single payer, albeit with regionally organised outposts.

On the delivery side, the patterns range from highly

centralised, government-dominated systems in Poland and Hungary to a rather decentralised Czech system which has a significant number of privately run hospitals.

There are also great differences in waiting times and access to modern technologies. Waiting lists are often unofficial and unmanaged, which encourages the under-the-table payments mentioned above. The extent of the grey economy is, of course, hard to quantify, but indirect measures point to its significance and to a negative correlation with the current level of funding and competition in the system.

Health reform is a hot political issue in all of these countries. However, so far only Slovakia has started producing any real remedies. The Slovak parliament adopted brand-new health legislation at the end of 2004. The extent and depth of the changes has made Slovakia a frontrunner in market-oriented health reforms, not only among new member states, but also in Europe overall. The implemented changes include the introduction of user charges, an explicit definition of the basic benefit package covered by statutory health insurance, for-profit status of health insurers and providers, and selective purchasing of care by insurers. These reforms have already led to a sharp reduction in the annual health system deficit.

In the Czech Republic, Hungary and Poland, reform has been put on hold until the next elections, all of which are planned for 2006. However, a reform similar to the Slovak one seems inevitable. In the past decade, all of these countries have to a large extent copied western European healthcare systems. But they do not have the deep pockets to feed them. The lack of individual responsibility these systems evoke, in combination with less efficient public institutions than in the west, are bringing them close to bankruptcy even before population ageing strikes with its full strength.

Old Europe versus new

The group of new member states we polled clearly differs from the 'old' Europe on many performance indicators, while scoring close to the average on values-related indicators.

Starting with the values, when it comes to prioritising equality of treatment for all over the quality of treatment received by individuals and their families, there is no clear difference between the old and new member states. Citizens across Europe – old and new – consider fairness and equality of access to be a very high priority.

On the other hand, citizens of the new member states are strongly persuaded that their systems are not able to fulfil their expectations. With the exception of the Czech Republic, all of them occupy the highest rankings in the Delivery Deficit, accompanied only by Britain, with its state-run, state-funded National Health Service.

It is apparent that those in the NMS4 have a more negative view of their healthcare systems on average than those living in the EU7 and the survey as a whole. Slovakia, Poland and Hungary are among the four worst-performing healthcare systems as measured by the Delivery Deficit. Only the Czech Republic, at 54%, performs better than the survey average of 55%, and only one EU7 country, Britain (63%), fails to perform better than the NMS4 average (63%). In contrast, the EU7 average Delivery Deficit is 50%. This should be a wake-up call not only for politicians in the new member states, but also – and especially – for the British government. When voters and

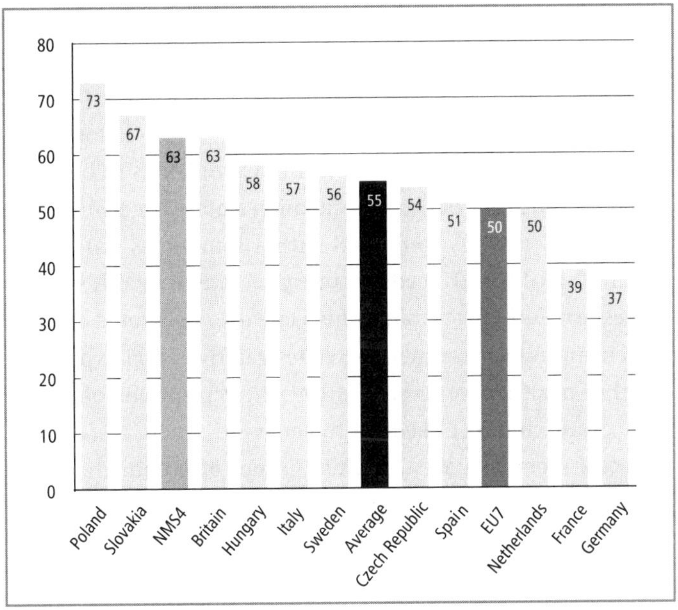

Figure 1 **Delivery Deficit**

Difference between what people want from healthcare and what they get

commentators compare the NHS to a communist system, it seems they really mean it.

The gap between expectations and reality is the highest on access (time between diagnosis and treatment), followed by convenience (being treated at a time and place to suit you) and provision of information.

Indeed, there is often a real issue with access – and not just in the case of the latest technologies. While healthcare systems in western Europe already have some problems with waiting lists and rationing of expensive new treatments and medicines (and there will be many more problems on the horizon), judged by mere provision of necessary care they mostly work quite well. This is not always so in the new member states.

Ranking on absolute performance is closely followed by relative performance. The 'Inferiority Complex' is to be taken literally in the case of the new member states. The real state of their health systems combined with a sometimes unfounded admiration of the EU leads to a rosy picture of health systems in western Europe, although this view may be altered as more citizens from the new member states gain personal experience of other health systems within the EU. Perceptions of performance are closely linked with perceived levels of funding. The new member states certainly do not give enough money to their health professionals. If they did, the systems would almost certainly perform better than they do at present.

Underfunding at home

The NMS4 states occupy the top places among those countries who believe on balance that their health systems have too little money. Among NMS4 countries as a whole, 73% think their healthcare systems are underfunded, 18% say they are adequately funded and just 4% believe they have too much money. The majority who therefore think that healthcare in the NMS4 countries is inadequately resourced is 51%.

Among EU7 countries only Sweden has a similar sized majority believing this – perhaps ironically, given the well-known generosity of the Swedish welfare state! The average majority in EU7 states claiming that healthcare is underfunded is less than half the NMS4 average at 24%.

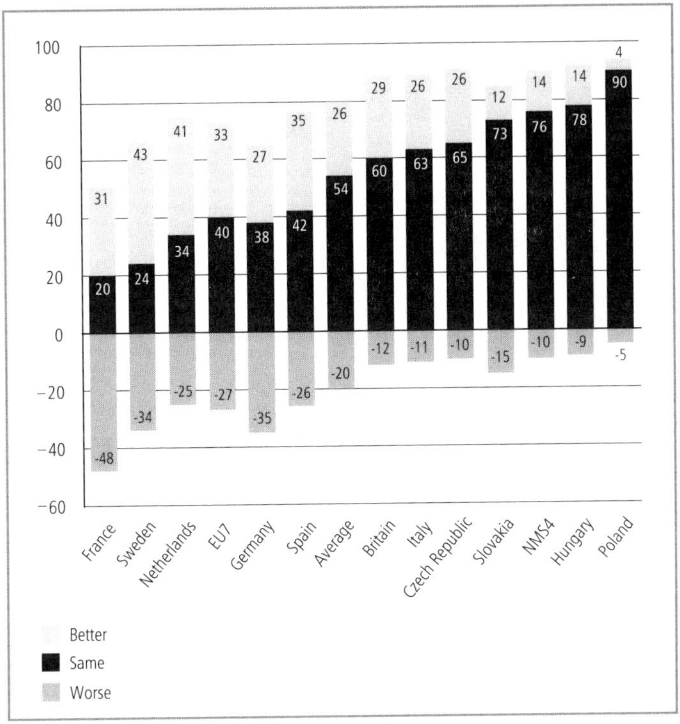

Figure 2 **Inferiority Complex**

How do other European health systems perform compared with your own?

Prospects for reform

The delivery and funding gaps are very well reflected in readiness for reform. The new member states fill four out of the five top positions. So far the results bring no surprise to a reader from western Europe. Now comes the surprise: why do more citizens in the new member states than in 'old' Europe expect the performance of their systems to improve even without

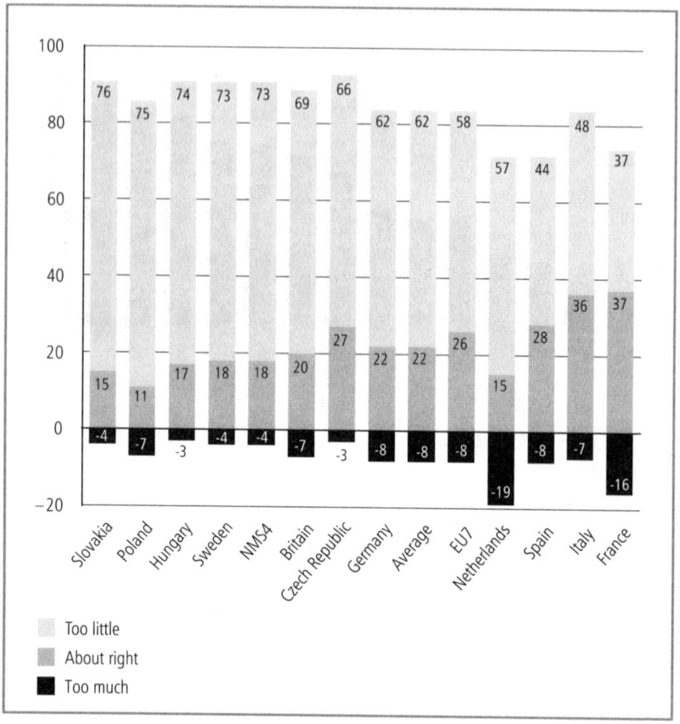

Figure 3 Underfunding at home

How much money does your health system have?

reform? What is the source of their relative optimism? There is actually more to this finding than may be apparent at first sight.

First, in many cases the starting point is very low, so there is a lot of space for improvement. Second, there are examples of significant improvements in quality and accessibility of other services and products witnessed in the new member states in the past few years. Third, and maybe most importantly, extra cash is flowing into health services due to relatively fast economic growth in the new member states. So, after all, central and eastern European citizens of the new member states may be right to expect some marginal improvements to their health systems even without reform. The question is whether they will have the patience to wait or whether they will demand signifi-

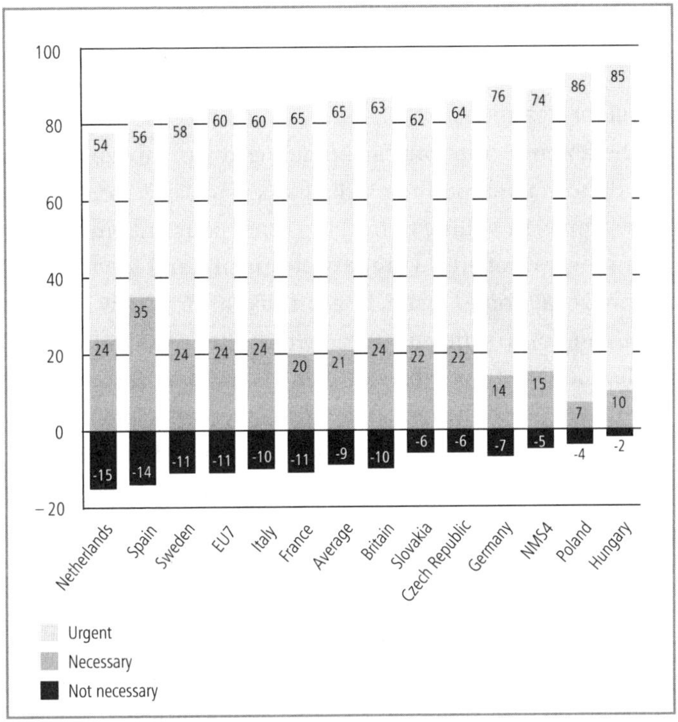

Figure 4 **Reform Index**

Does your healthcare system need reforming?

cant improvements right now. The latter response seems more likely, given that 74% of respondents view reform as being urgent and 59% of them are persuaded that without any reform their health systems will get worse, even with the extra cash.

Rather than differing widely, when it comes to the desire for reform, it seems that the east is just as impatient for change as the west, if not more so. As a group, the NMS4 scored an average Reform Index rating of 84%, higher than any single EU7 country and comfortably higher than the EU7 average of 73%.

Travel for treatment

In the absence of reform at home, what can citizens in the east do to get around their lack of access to care? Would they, for example, be willing to travel to other parts of Europe to be seen sooner or offered a range of treatments and services they cannot get at home? Again, it seems that the four new member states are not so different from their counterparts in the west. Willingness to travel for treatment is, on average, not very different between the new and old member states and seems to be closely correlated to real and perceived underfunding. Some 69% of people in NMS4 countries say they would travel abroad for treatment, if their healthcare systems paid for it, against 27% who would not. This compares with EU7 countries where a majority would be willing to go abroad by 64% to 33%.

The Poles and Slovaks are more ready to travel than their counterparts in the Czech Republic and Hungary, who enjoy better access to health services due to significantly higher levels of funding. The same seems to be true for travel-ready Swedes and Britons, who have long waiting lists and higher levels of

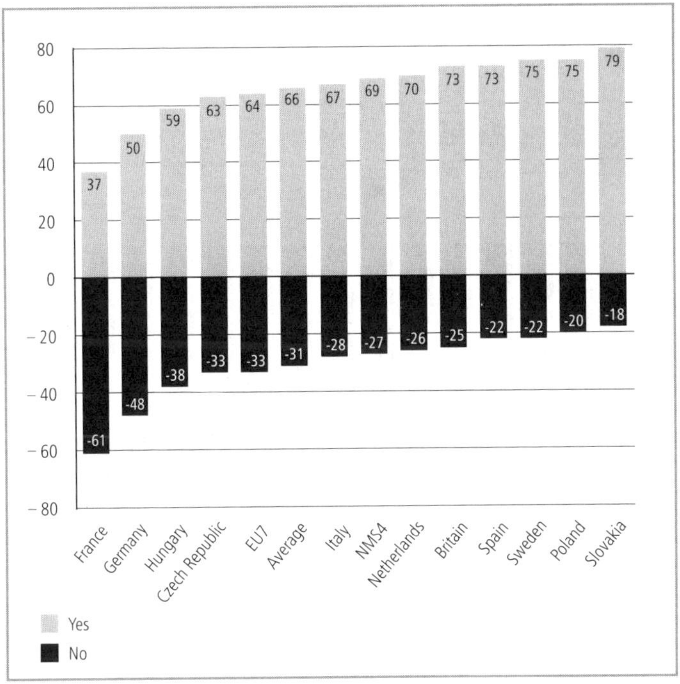

Figure 5 **Travel for treatment**

Would you travel abroad for treatment if your health system paid?

rationing. Meanwhile, the 'conservative' Germans and French, who have historically had the best-funded and most generous health systems in the EU and, crucially, are unfamiliar with waiting lists, are, perhaps not surprisingly, happier to stay at home.

A rosy future?

The picture is more mixed when people are asked to consider

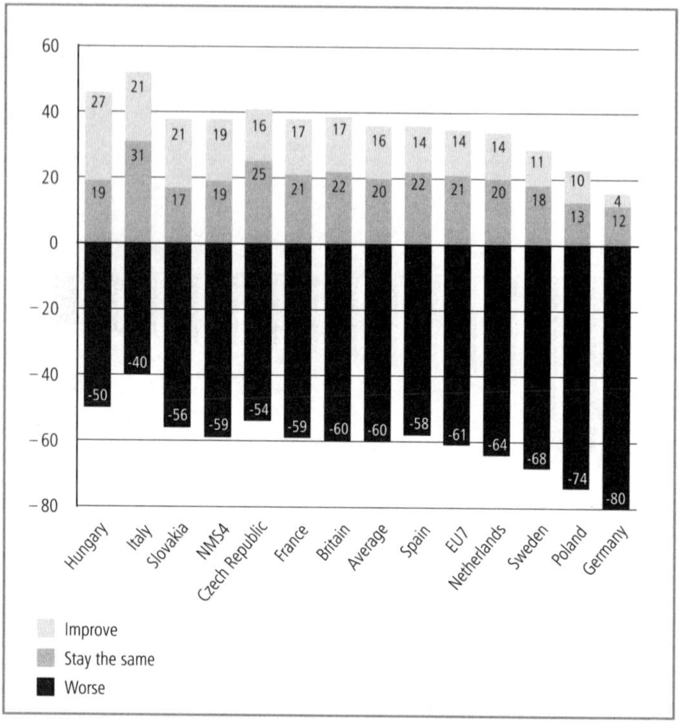

Figure 6 Pessimism Ranking

Prospects for healthcare in ten years' time if your system remains unreformed

the prospects for healthcare in their country over the next decade in the absence of reform. Here, three of the NMS4, Hungary, Slovakia and the Czech Republic, are among the least pessimistic states surveyed, though Poland's pessimism about the future of its current healthcare system is surpassed only by Germany. This is relative, though. On average, 59% of people in the NMS4 think that healthcare will get worse in the absence of reform, 19% think it will stay the same, and a further 19% think it will actually improve. This gives the NMS4 a Pessimism Ranking of 59%. Of the EU7 countries, only Italy, with a Pessimism Ranking of 50%, is more optimistic, whereas the EU7 average is 68%.

Steps forward

Given the low performance rankings of current systems in the east and the readiness for change of would-be political reformers, the new member states should be in a good starting position to enact major changes to their systems in the years ahead. But what do their citizens actually expect them to do in the areas of funding and delivery of services, and will they trust their intentions?

Where should the extra money for healthcare come from, for example? Citizens in the new member states clearly share their western counterparts' illusion of a 'free lunch' gained by shifting higher healthcare costs on to business. However, putting this idea of improving care at someone else's expense aside, people in the new member states are considerably less supportive of higher taxation and, at least in the Czech Republic and Hungary, more prepared to pay more out of their pockets.

Besides increased funding, what do they believe would lead to increased quality of care? With the exception of Hungary, all countries surveyed point to giving patients more health information as the most powerful tool. Perhaps surprisingly, they put increasing the number of medicines and treatments, as well as increasing the range of doctors and hospitals, lowest in the range of needed reforms and so do not differ markedly from their western counterparts, despite some real problems with access to care. This is especially surprising in the case of Poland, where citizens have not been reimbursed for the newest medicines for the past eight years. It also, however, no doubt reflects a time lag in expectations between east and west.

As yet, the new member states are not accustomed to high levels of service or access to new therapies, and are therefore likely to have more realistic expectations (or be more accepting) than their western neighbours. Patient groups, for example, which are now a common phenomenon in the rest of the EU, tend to drive up expectations and awareness of new treatments for particular diseases, and to exert additional pressure on politicians to make them available. Such groups are only beginning to be established in the new member states and, as they emerge, may well drive up patient demand.

There is no doubt that the required reforms will be painful, at least in the beginning. Who will then be able to persuade citizens to bear the burden? Politicians seem to be a lost cause, being trusted even less in the new Europe than in the old member states. The favourite sources of information on healthcare, besides citizens' own experience, are health professionals. Official statistics and NGOs are also not to be underestimated in future, especially given the current lack of useful content and user-friendly format of government reports and the relative underdevelopment of NGOS in the east at present. Once such groups start publishing reliable and understandable information on quality of care, they are likely to be gratefully accepted by the public.

Addressing the question of who should help them to keep themselves healthy, people in the new member states rely slightly more on physicians and less on government than is the pattern in western Europe. This again demonstrates the crucial role of the medical profession and underscores its importance in public acceptance of any reform proposals. The good news for reformers in the new member states is that their physicians might be more reform-minded, due to their financial status, which lags significantly behind that of their relatively well-paid western European colleagues.

Summing up, the main differences in opinion between the 'new' and the 'old' Europe seem to be caused by differences in access, due to significantly lower levels of funding, and by a sometimes unfounded admiration of western Europe. Yet the challenges facing healthcare systems and the way people view them are remarkably similar across the board. The likely outlook is that health reforms in the new member states may well go on to provide valuable inspiration and experience for policy experts in western Europe. Poles apart, then? No, not really.

part 2

Populus national polls and commentaries

Hungary

Hungary

Poll and analysis

Rick Nye

Context

Most important features of healthcare and health system's ability to deliver them

	Important	*Good*	*Net*
The time between diagnosis and treatment	97	20	77
Being treated at a time and a place to suit you	99	28	71
Having enough information to make an informed choice about your treatment	98	39	59
Being treated using the latest medicines/technology	82	30	52
Being treated by a doctor of your choice	90	60	30
Average delivery deficit			**58**

Which is more important to you about your health system?
(Solidarity Gap)

	Equality of access	*Quality of personal care*	*Net*
Hungary	88	11	77
Netherlands	84	15	69
Italy	84	15	69
Spain	83	17	66
Sweden	81	17	64
Germany	81	18	63
Czech Republic	81	18	63
Average	**80**	**18**	**62**
Slovakia	80	18	62
France	78	21	57
Poland	75	20	55
Britain	69	31	38

How do other European health systems perform compared with your own? (Inferiority Complex)

	Better	*The same*	*Worse*	*Better minus the same/worse*
Poland	90	4	5	80
Hungary	78	14	9	55
Slovakia	73	12	15	46
Czech Republic	65	26	10	28
Italy	63	26	11	26
Britain	60	29	12	19
Average	**54**	**26**	**20**	**8**
Spain	42	35	26	–19
Germany	38	27	35	–24
Netherlands	34	41	25	–32
Sweden	24	43	34	–53
France	20	31	48	–59

Health System: marks out of 10

France	6.9	**Average**	**5.6**
Netherlands	6.7	Czech Republic	5.3
Spain	6.7	Germany	5.1
Britain	5.9	Hungary	5.1
Sweden	5.8	Slovakia	4.4
Italy	5.8	Poland	3.8

Prospects for healthcare in 10 years' time if your system remains unreformed (Pessimism Ranking)

	Improve	*Stay the same*	*Get worse*	*Stay the same/get worse minus improve*
Germany	4	12	80	88
Poland	10	13	74	77
Sweden	11	18	68	75
Netherlands	14	20	64	70
Spain	14	22	58	66
Average	**16**	**20**	**60**	**65**
Britain	17	22	60	65
France	17	21	59	63
Czech Republic	16	25	54	63
Slovakia	21	17	56	52
Italy	21	31	40	50
Hungary	27	19	50	42

Does your health system need reforming? (Reform Index)

	Yes (urgently)	*Yes*	*No*	*Yes (urgently)/yes minus no*
Hungary	85	10	2	93
Poland	86	7	4	89
Germany	76	14	7	83
Czech Republic	64	22	6	80
Slovakia	62	22	6	78
Britain	63	24	10	77
Average	**65**	**21**	**9**	**77**
France	65	20	11	74
Italy	60	24	10	74
Sweden	58	24	11	71
Spain	46	35	14	67
Netherlands	54	24	15	63

Analysis

More people in Hungary believe their healthcare system needs reforming than in any other country surveyed. They think the Hungarian system performs poorly compared to the health systems of other countries – only Poland is less confident about its own system relative to its neighbours' – and specifically in terms of the gap between aspiration and delivery. Here Hungary is below the survey average and betters only Britain, Slovakia and Poland in that regard. Despite this, Hungarians claim to be less pessimistic than any other nation surveyed about the prospects for their healthcare system in the absence of reform over the next ten years. A larger majority also backs equality of access over quality of personal care in Hungary than in any other country. Overall, Hungarians mark their health system at 5.1 out of 10, the same as Germany and ahead only of Slovakia and Poland among the eleven EU nations in this study.

More than four out of five Hungarians (85%) say that their healthcare system is in need of urgent reform, the highest proportion of any country surveyed apart from Poland. This includes nine out of ten (90%) of 35–44-year-olds, though only just over three-quarters (76%) of over-65s. A further 10% say reform is necessary. One in six (16%) of 15–24-year-olds say this. And just 2% say reform is unnecessary, rising to 7% among the over-65s. Hungary therefore has a 'Reform Index' rating of 93%, the highest of any nation studied in the survey.

Hungarians also think their health system performs poorly compared with those of other countries. Of those expressing a view, more than three-quarters (78%) think other countries' healthcare systems perform better, one in seven (14%) believe they perform to a similar standard, and less than one in ten (9%) think they perform worse. This gives Hungary an 'Inferiority Complex' of 55%, the second highest of the eleven countries studied, behind Poland.

This is in part because Hungarians believe their healthcare system to be underfunded in both absolute and relative terms. Nearly three quarters (74%) say their system has too little money, including more than four out of five (82%) 15–24-year-olds, but only three out of five (61%) people over the age of 65. One in six Hungarians (17%) say their healthcare system is adequately funded, including more than a quarter (27%) of over-65s, and just 3% say it has too much money.

Comparing Hungarian levels of funding with those in

other countries, more than four out of five (82%) expressing an opinion say other nations have more to spend on health – the highest proportion outside Poland – against fewer than one in seven (13%) who believe that Hungary has more to spend. Despite this, Hungarians are more opposed to increasing personal taxes to pay for extra healthcare spending than any other country surveyed. Just 4% believe this is the most appropriate route, compared with nearly half (46%) who would like to see the money come from higher costs on business and one in five (19%) who favour higher personal spending.

Nevertheless, a larger number of Hungarians place equality of access for everyone ahead of quality of care for themselves and their family than in any other country surveyed. Some 88% do this – including 92% of over-65s – against 11% who put quality first. This gives Hungary a 'Solidarity Gap' rating of 77%, comfortably top of the eleven EU countries surveyed.

Half of Hungarians (50%) believe that the quality of healthcare in their country will get worse in the absence of reform, ranging from just over a third (36%) of 15–24-year-olds and two out of five (42%) among the over-65s, to nearly three out of five (59%) 55–64-year-olds. However, more than a quarter (27%) of Hungarians believe that healthcare will actually improve in the absence of reform, while 19% say standards will remain the same. This gives Hungary a 'Pessimism Ranking' of 42%, the lowest level of net pessimism among any of the countries in the study. Hungarians are also reluctant to travel for treatment abroad, relatively speaking. Though a majority would do so by 59% to 38%, this majority is slimmer than in any country surveyed other than Germany and France (where a majority would choose to stay at home). Three-quarters of Hungarians

(76%) aged 15–24 would travel abroad for treatment, but less than a third (31%) of over-65s would, with more than double the number (65%) opting to stay at home.

When it comes to the specific performance measures used to calculate the 'Delivery Deficit', the priorities of Hungarians are similar to those of people in the other countries surveyed. As many as 99% rate being treated at a time and place to suit them as being important – the highest proportion of any country surveyed and above the average of 91%. Hungarians also place slightly greater store by being treated by a doctor of their choice (90% say this is important, against an average of 86%). But they place marginally less emphasis on being treated with the latest medicines and technology (82% say this is important, against an average of 88%)

On ranking the ability of the Hungarian healthcare system to deliver on these priorities, only one in five (20%) say it is good on the time taken between diagnosis and treatment, while slightly more than a quarter (28%) say it performs well on treating people at a time and place to suit them, and two out of five (39%) say it is good at giving patients enough information about their treatment. Hungarian healthcare scores best, however, on delivering doctor choice. Three out of five (60%) think it is good in this regard. Overall, Hungary has a Delivery Deficit rating of 58%, eighth out of the eleven countries surveyed, compared with the average of 55% and ahead of Britain, Slovakia and Poland.

More people in Hungary than in any other country believe that increasing the number of medicines and treatments available to patients will improve quality of care. Four out of five (79%) people say this, including 84% of 15–24-year-olds.

Reforms most likely to increase the quality of care

	Likely	*Not likely*	*Net*
Increasing number of medicines and treatments	79	16	63
Increasing range of doctors and hospitals	65	31	34
Giving patients more information about their illness	62	33	29
Making it easier for patients to spend their own money on health	53	36	17
Giving patients more control over public spending on health	38	55	–17

The next most popular reform is increasing the number of doctors and hospitals, and by a two-to-one majority (65% to 31%) Hungarians believe this would also improve the quality of care, with 45–54-year-olds especially thinking so (by 70% to 26%). More patient information is favoured, by 62% to 33%. It is a reform slightly more popular among younger Hungarians (35–44-year-olds back it by 70% to 24%) than older ones (the over-65s favour it by 57% to 34%). The majority favouring making it easier for patients to spend their own money on health (53% to 36%) is higher than in any country except Britain and the Czech Republic. 35–44-year-olds are particularly keen in this regard, favouring the measure by 62% to 28%. Older Hungarians are more sceptical, and a majority of over-65s actually oppose it by 44% to 40%. Giving patients more control over public spending on health meets with less favour among Hungarians than among people in any other country surveyed. By a margin of 55% to 38%, Hungarians think this is unlikely to increase the quality of healthcare. 35–44-year-

Most reliable sources of health information (Credibility Gap)

	Reliable	Unreliable	Net
Experience	87	9	78
Doctors/nurses	86	9	77
NGOs	59	18	41
Official statistics	56	38	18
Industry	49	38	11
Media	48	49	–1
Politicians	26	68	–42

olds are particularly opposed (by 60% to 37%), whereas older Hungarians are more sympathetic, though still opposed by 34% to 47%.

When it comes to the relative reliability of sources of information, Hungarians are marginally more trusting than the average of countries surveyed. No country trusts the personal experiences of friends and family more than Hungarians. Some 87% of people do this, against only 9% who consider them unreliable. This gives a 'Credibility Gap' rating of +78% compared with an average rating of +63%. 86% of Hungarians trust the views of doctors and nurses while 9% do not, a Credibility Gap of +77%, broadly in line with the average of +74%. Non-governmental organisations also score highly as sources of healthcare information. Nearly three-fifths of Hungarians (59%) trust them, as opposed to 18% who don't. NGOs' Credibility Gap is therefore +41% (average +41%). A majority also believes what the healthcare industry has to say by 49% to 38%, a Credibility Gap of +11% (average +16%). Hungary is also in line with general sentiment about the reliability of official statistics, which are believed by a majority of 56% to 38%, a Credibility Gap of +18% (average +17%). Almost as many people believe media stories as do not, 48% against 49%. The media has a Credibility Gap of –1% (average –4%). Finally, politicians fare badly in absolute terms, but do better relatively in Hungary than in most other countries. They are distrusted by a margin of 68% to 26%, giving them a Credibility Gap of –42%, somewhat better than the survey average of –60%.

When it comes to taking greater personal responsibility for keeping healthy, 99% of Hungarians think they should do this, the highest proportion in the survey along with Poland. 44% think doctors have the greatest role to play in helping them, and 28% think this is primarily the responsibility of government, both in line with the average of the eleven countries surveyed.

Summary

Hungary

Delivery Deficit	58	8th
Solidarity Gap	77	1st
Inferiority Complex	55	2nd
Marks out of 10	5.1	8th=
Pessimism Ranking	42	11th
Reform Index	93	1st

Hungary

Commentary

David Hill

Hungary has come a long way since 1989, before which healthcare – like everything else – was the domain of the state. The country has lots of efficient and well-equipped private clinics: a few big, many small. But the failings of its public hospital system – cash-starved, corrupt, even unhygienic – are the stuff of local legend. And in the absence of the political will to change things, health professionals say it is unlikely either that the public system will improve, or that private service providers will be able to take over much of the demand.

Hungarians are traditionally good at promoting themselves to the world as scientific experts, and the medical sector is no exception. Thousands of small clinics, typically offering dental, optical or cosmetic treatment, dot the country, largely earning their keep from the custom of foreigners, particularly Germans and Austrians. In many cases, these westerners combine visits to such places with a dip in Hungary's famous spa waters on a general 'wellness' trip.

When it comes to larger private clinics with a wide range of services, there are a good two dozen in and around Budapest, of which at least ten had revenues of more than 100 million Hungarian forints (about €400,000) in 2004. To put that in perspective, the Health Ministry's budget in 2005 is 141 billion forints. But these larger clinics, too, traditionally draw their patients primarily from among foreigners, in this case Hungary's large expatriate business community. The number of Hungarians using their services as paying customers is steadily increasing, but still low.

'A large portion of our patient base is expat families,' says Brian Chalmers, managing director of one of the biggest, FirstMed Centers Kft. 'Our local patient base is close to ten per cent or fifteen per cent of our total patients. The number of tourists we saw in the clinic rose dramatically last year due to the exponential increase of tourism in Budapest.'

Another source of revenue for private clinics, which some but not all of them use, is the outsourcing of public services. A patient can go to such a clinic to have an operation done as part of the public health provision, with the state paying the clinic for the procedure.

Kelen Hospital, founded in 1999 by two Hungarian owners, is one clinic which takes advantage of this possibility. Undertaking outpatient care and one-day surgery, it offers these services both on a totally private basis and under contract with the state system.

'We chose this arrangement hoping that state financing would increase, or that people, while coming here to have treatment financed by the state, would see what else we do and choose to have some private treatment as well,' explains

Randy Simor, business development director of Kelen.

But clinics receive only a fraction as much when a treatment is paid for by the state, as they do when a private paying client coughs up. So there remains little motivation for private clinics to eat away at the public market in this way.

In particular, doctors complain that the National Health Insurance Fund is unsympathetic when some new, better type of surgery costs more than the procedure hitherto used to treat the same complaint. They say the fund is reluctant to shell out the incremental amount. 'It's like someone refusing to pay more for an electric light than for a candle because they both do the same job,' complains Sarolta Baricza, the medical director of Kelen.

In the midst of all this, the public hospital system, which is mandated to provide universal state-funded care, is chronically indebted and inefficient. Oft-mentioned scenarios include hospitalised patients having to bring their own soap and toilet paper into the ward, or their relatives coming in and scrubbing the ward themselves to ensure cleanliness. Yet the average Hungarian remains staunchly in favour of a free national healthcare system.

In the present constitution, which dates back to 1989, health services are available to all citizens universally. Local governments are responsible for arranging for the delivery of public healthcare services, while financing comes centrally from the National Health Insurance Fund. Citizens pay obligatory contributions into the kitty, calculated on the basis of solidarity – that is, as a proportion of income, not in proportion to their individual risk. But while overwhelmingly in favour of this solidarity-based system, Hungarian patients are paradoxically willing to engage in the endemic practice of paying additional doctors' fees under the table. Though paid in advance, these tips are euphemistically known as *hálapénz*, or 'gratitude money'.

This practice is so widely accepted that it is even mentioned on the website of the Ministry of Health, Social and Family Affairs. 'Informal gratitude payments can be estimated at some 1–3% of total healthcare expenditure,' says the site. Independent researchers estimated that in 2003 the tips totalled 30 billion forints, with 87% going to doctors and 13% to nurses.

Representatives of the private sector are quick to point out the irony of this situation. If a hospital is private, very few people are willing to pay the money to be treated there, but they will happily pay gratitude money in a public hospital.

'There has been so much criticism of the privatisation of healthcare lately, and nobody is talking about how [gratitude money] is exactly that. Patients, in addition to paying their health tax, are paying extra money for better service,' says Chalmers.

Other conflicts abound in the public health system. For example, some patients complain of doctors being in the pay of drug companies to push pills. The health ministry, too, has repeatedly complained that the subsidies it is obliged to pay out for prescription drugs add up to an excessively large amount, and alleges that doctors are prescribing too many, too expensive drugs. Meanwhile, patients often find themselves strong-armed to stay longer in hospital than is really necessary, as hospitals' financing is calculated partly on the basis of how many beds are occupied. The ministry website complains of the 'hospital-centred structure' of Hungarian healthcare, alleging that 'very often and without any specific reason, care takes place at the highest and most costly level of the system instead of primary healthcare or outpatient care.' And all the while, health workers regularly protest over low wages.

In an attempt to bring private capital into the cash-starved system, some of Hungary's post-1989 governments – in particular, ironically, the ones led by the Socialist party – have tried to encourage investors to buy the right to run state hospitals. The investors are expected to pump their own money into making the hospitals more efficient, and continue to provide the services mandated by law, with the paying customer being the state. In such scenarios, the private operation has to be set up as a not-for-profit company.

Given the limited attractions to investors, a tiny handful of hospitals in the country have been 'privatised' in this way, with the buyers sometimes being the medical staff themselves, concerned about keeping their place of employment going. 'Why would private capital want to go into this market? The government says patients have to get certain services, but it will only pay so much,' says Simor.

And yet the mere mention of such deals being possible has been enough for certain political forces to arouse public fury against supposed attempts to make a business out of what most Hungarians feel should be a socialised system.

Notably, the non-parliamentary Workers Party, joined in an unholy alliance by the supposedly right-wing main opposition party, Fidesz, called a referendum in December 2004, asking whether the 'privatisation' should stop. While the turnout was only 37.4% – well short of the 50% needed for the vote to have validity – 65% of people who did vote were in favour of stopping the inflow of private capital. So, while Hungary's

10 million people are in general unsatisfied with the quality of healthcare they receive, and the minority who can afford it are happy to use private clinics, there continues to be a strong feeling that state-funded care should be available for all.

This would be a perfectly good model, say health professionals, if only the government were prepared to pump more money into the system. That includes settling hospitals' ballooning debts, modernising the facilities, and paying doctors a lot more, to prevent them migrating to the private sector, or, increasingly, to western countries. 'The best solution is for the government to really bring in far-reaching reform – which would lead to more money,' Simor says. 'There must be increased salary for medical staff,' contends Chalmers.

And indeed, Hungary's public health spending is below the 8.5% EU average, hovering at around 6.5%. Yet, with the country hoping to adopt the euro, which means hacking its budget deficit down to 3% of GDP compared with last year's 5.1%, the money simply isn't there.

Which leaves another option – to encourage private clinics, so that more and more people will choose them, and unburden the public system, leaving it to take care of the most needy. And one missing link that could allow this to happen is the availability of private health insurance.

With no companies in Hungary offering such policies, there is likely to remain limited spending power for private healthcare. That perpetuates a vicious circle, because it means that investors are unwilling to enter the market and make private care more available. 'As soon as more people have access to private health insurance plans, more private facilities will be opened. More facilities means more competition, which improves the overall quality of the product and service, and ultimately reduces the cost of private care, as the costs are spread out over a larger patient base,' says Chalmers.

But there seems little likelihood of such insurance being offered to Hungarians in the near future. 'I think it will be some time before we see private health insurance develop in Hungary, mainly due to the prohibitively high cost of state health insurance. Additionally, the benefit tax for providing private health insurance adds to the overall costs,' says Chalmers. 'It's difficult for employers to pay into the compulsory state fund and then pay for private insurance on top.'

The government could help this situation if it promised that private health insurance clients would be exempt from paying contributions to the public system. Yet that would require a loss of central revenue and state control, a pill which successive governments have refused to swallow.

So, are Hungarians getting the healthcare they want? That is a tough question, because it is difficult to know what they really want. Hungarians' responses to the Stockholm Network-commissioned Populus poll indicate a readiness to complain about the present situation – yet a more muted enthusiasm when put on the spot about something actually being done about it. For example, Hungarians are the most adamant out of all the eleven nations that their health system needs reform. Yet when quizzed about what might happen to the system if it is not reformed, Hungarians are the most likely to think that it might get better if just left alone.

Similarly, when asked about their impressions of other countries' health systems, 78% of Hungarians said they are convinced that foreigners enjoy better care – the second highest figure, after Poland. Nevertheless, asked whether they would travel abroad for treatment, Hungarians emerged as the third-least-likely people to do so, after the French and the Germans.

It's often said that if you ask a Hungarian how he or she is, instead of an automatic 'fine, thanks,' you will get a literal answer, detailing a list of ailments. However, local doctors note, Hungarians are slow to make constructive criticisms in specific areas where improvements could be made. That includes a surprising deference toward the medical profession.

'Hungarian patients are not as sensitive to quality as westerners. They kind of accept what's been thrown at them. Western patients are constantly second-opinioning,' says Simor, who is familiar with both Hungarian and American patient habits. Perhaps hand-in-hand with this goes the docile acceptance with which patients slip doctors gratitude money, without asking for a receipt or an explanation of how this payment will improve the treatment. At the same time, the ability to choose doctors or clinics, or the requirement to get high-quality treatment, are not top priorities for Hungarian healthcare consumers.

The Populus poll found that a majority of Hungarians consider equality of access for all to be more important than the quality of personal care they themselves receive. Indeed, with 88% of people valuing that criterion, and only 11% putting quality first, the gap is the largest of all the eleven EU countries in which Populus conducted the poll. 'The few people who are informed have higher expectations, but the bulk of the population just want care to be the same for everyone,' agrees Baricza at Kelen.

Besides all this, health ministry statistics reveal that Hungarians could do with being more self-critical when it comes to maintaining their own well-being. Hungarians consume too much fat, cholesterol, sugar and salt, and not enough fibre, vegetables and fruits, according to the ministry's website. They also drink and smoke too much, and 'the physical activity of the population in leisure time is not more than ten minutes a day.'

These lifestyle problems are reflected in the prevalent ailments in Hungary. Obesity affects more than 1.5 million people. Deaths related to smoking were nearly 2.5 times higher than the EU average in the late 1990s, and Hungary has the highest rate of death by lung cancer in Europe. In 2000, mortality due to excess alcohol consumption was more than three times as high as the EU average for males, and two and a half times higher for females. In 2001, 439,000 patients were treated in hospitals due to diseases of the circulatory system, while hypertension is also high. And more than 15% of the population has severe depression at least once in their lives. The bone density figures of the Hungarian population are the lowest in Europe.

A separate report on the state of Hungarians' health in 2003 found that 26% of women and 40% of men smoke. Yet it also found that, while lifestyle factors play a role in one-third of all illnesses, 33% of women and 25% of men believe there is nothing they can do for better health.

So, are Hungarian healthcare users impatient for change? Certainly there is widespread dissatisfaction, with most people longing for cradle-to-grave care and comfort, which they are simply not getting. But they are never going to feel better until they start being more specifically demanding of their doctors and themselves – and until the government has the guts to create conditions in which both the public and private sectors can improve.

With thousands of extremely competent, well-trained medics, and with a universally recognised need for some kind of improvement, it's certain that the potential, at least, is there.

Poland

Poland

Poll and analysis

Rick Nye

Context

Most important features of healthcare and health system's ability to deliver them

	Important	*Good*	*Net*
The time between diagnosis and treatment	98	12	86
Being treated at a time and a place to suit you	96	20	76
Having enough information to make an informed choice about your treatment	96	24	72
Being treated using the latest medicines/technology	95	22	73
Being treated by a doctor of your choice	95	38	57
Average delivery deficit			73

Which is more important to you about your health system?
(Solidarity Gap)

	Equality of access	*Quality of personal care*	*Net*
Hungary	88	11	77
Netherlands	84	15	69
Italy	84	15	69
Spain	83	17	66
Sweden	81	17	64
Germany	81	18	63
Czech Republic	81	18	63
Average	**80**	**18**	**62**
Slovakia	80	18	62
France	78	21	57
Poland	75	20	55
Britain	69	31	38

How do other European health systems perform compared with your own? (Inferiority Complex)

	Better	*The same*	*Worse*	*Better minus the same/worse*
Poland	90	4	5	80
Hungary	78	14	9	55
Slovakia	73	12	15	46
Czech Republic	65	26	10	28
Italy	63	26	11	26
Britain	60	29	12	19
Average	**54**	**26**	**20**	**8**
Spain	42	35	26	–19
Germany	38	27	35	–24
Netherlands	34	41	25	–32
Sweden	24	43	34	–53
France	20	31	48	–59

Health System: marks out of 10

France	6.9	**Average**	**5.6**
Netherlands	6.7	Czech Republic	5.3
Spain	6.7	Germany	5.1
Britain	5.9	Hungary	5.1
Sweden	5.8	Slovakia	4.4
Italy	5.8	Poland	3.8

Prospects for healthcare in 10 years' time if your system remains unreformed (Pessimism Ranking)

	Improve	*Stay the same*	*Get worse*	*Stay the same/get worse minus improve*
Germany	4	12	80	88
Poland	10	13	74	77
Sweden	11	18	68	75
Netherlands	14	20	64	70
Spain	14	22	58	66
Average	**16**	**20**	**60**	**65**
Britain	17	22	60	65
France	17	21	59	63
Czech Republic	16	25	54	63
Slovakia	21	17	56	52
Italy	21	31	40	50
Hungary	27	19	50	42

Does your health system need reforming? (Reform Index)

	Yes (urgently)	*Yes*	*No*	*Yes (urgently)/yes minus no*
Hungary	85	10	2	93
Poland	86	7	4	89
Germany	76	14	7	83
Czech Republic	64	22	6	80
Slovakia	62	22	6	78
Britain	63	24	10	77
Average	**65**	**21**	**9**	**77**
France	65	20	11	74
Italy	60	24	10	74
Sweden	58	24	11	71
Spain	46	35	14	67
Netherlands	54	24	15	63

Analysis

Poles rank their health system as the worst of all the eleven EU countries studied. They give it the lowest overall mark, 3.8 out of 10, a full 0.6 behind the next lowest ranked country, Slovakia. On the overall measure of performance against aspiration, Poland again comes bottom, by some distance. And only one in seven Poles say their health system is good at meeting individual needs, the lowest proportion of any country surveyed. Unsurprisingly, then, Poles have the lowest regard for their healthcare system relative to those in other countries, and in no other country does a greater proportion of people think that other nations have more to spend on health. More people in Poland also think that healthcare reform is urgent than in any other country surveyed, and more people in Poland believe that health standards will deteriorate in the absence of reform than in any country other than Germany.

More than four in five Poles (86%) say that healthcare reform is urgent in their country – the highest proportion of any country surveyed. This includes 90% of 35–44-year-olds, dropping to 80% of those aged 65 or over. A further 7% say reform is necessary. One in eight (12%) of 15–24-year-olds say this, as do one in nine (11%) of over-65s. Only 4% of Poles believe reform is unnecessary, the lowest proportion in any country with the exception of Hungary. This gives Poland a 'Reform Index' rating of 89%, compared with an average of 77%, and second only to Hungary's 93%.

Three-quarters of Poles (74%) say that healthcare will deteriorate over the next ten years without reform, second only to Germany. More than four out of five (84%) of people aged 35–44 believe this, compared with just over two-thirds (69%) of 15–24-year-olds and a similar number (68%) of 55–64-year-olds. One in eight Poles (13%) think standards will remain the same, ranging from 7% of over-65s to nearly one in five (18%) of 55–64-year-olds. Just one in ten (10%) say standards will actually rise in the absence of reform, the lowest proportion after Germany. This gives Poland a 'Pessimism Ranking' of 77%, compared to the survey average of 65% and places it second to Germany's 88% out of the eleven EU countries polled.

Three-quarters of Poles (75%) view their health system as underfunded, the highest proportion surveyed outside Slovakia. This ranges from more than four out of five (82%) of

15–24-year-olds to just over two-thirds (68%) of 55–64-year-olds. Just 11% think the Polish health system is adequately funded – the lowest proportion of any country surveyed – and a further 7% think it has too much money. The majority of Poles who believe that their healthcare system is therefore underfunded in absolute terms is matched only by Slovakia among the countries surveyed. In relative terms, however, no one surpasses Poland in believing that their healthcare system is underfunded relative to other countries. Of those prepared to express a view, nearly nine out of ten (88%) think other countries have more to spend on health than their own country – the highest proportion in any nation surveyed. Just 5% think they have the same amount of money and a mere 7% believe that Poland has more to spend, in both cases the lowest proportion in any of the eleven countries surveyed.

Despite this, Poles are near the survey average in believing that extra funding from health should come from higher personal taxation. One in five (19%) say this, ranging from a quarter (24%) of 15–24-year-olds to fewer than one in six (15%) of 55–64-year-olds. Only one in nine Poles (11%) are in favour of meeting the shortfall through higher personal spending, the lowest proportion outside Spain, ranging from 16% of 55–64-year-olds to just 5% of over-65s.

When it comes to relative performance, fully nine out of ten Poles (90%) expressing a view believe that other countries' health care systems outperform their own. Only 4% believe that standards are comparable and just 5% think that standards are worse elsewhere. The majority in Poland who believe that standards are better elsewhere, the measure used to derive its 'Inferiority Complex', is 80%, ten times as high as the survey average of 8% and comfortably higher than Hungary's 55% in second place.

Perhaps unsurprisingly, Poles are among the keenest to seek treatment abroad, providing their health system is prepared to pay for it. They are prepared to do so by a majority of 75% to 20%, ranging from 90% to 10% among 15–24-year-olds to 56% to 36% among the over-65s – the highest margin among any country surveyed except Slovakia.

In general, the Polish population regards its health system as poor at meeting individual needs. Only 14% of Poles rate their health system as good in this regard, compared with 20% who say it is fair. Both of these figures are the lowest in any country surveyed. However nearly two thirds (64%) say that it is poor at meeting individual needs, almost twice the proportion of the next most critical country, Hungary, where 34% say this. When it comes to the individual measures of healthcare quality used to determine the 'Delivery Deficit', Poland comes bottom in every regard. In no other country does a greater proportion of the population think that doctor choice is more important – 95% say this, compared with an average of 86% – and yet only 38% say their health system is good in this regard, ahead of only Britain, where 31% do so. On being treated at a time and place to suit them, a mere 20% of Poles say their health system performs well, even though 96% say waiting times are important. And on waiting times only 12% rate the Polish system as good, half the average of 23%, even though 98% of Poles say this is important. This story is repeated on using the latest medicines and technology, where only 22% say their system is good – again the lowest proportion of countries surveyed – while 95% say it is important, and on having enough information

Reforms most likely to increase the quality of care

	Likely	*Not likely*	*Net*
Giving patients more information about their illness	79	16	63
Increasing number of medicines and treatments	70	25	45
Increasing range of doctors and hospitals	53	42	11
Making it easier for patients to spend their own money on health	52	41	11
Giving patients more control over public spending on health	48	46	2

about their treatment which 96% rate as important, but only 24% of Poles rate as good under their system. Overall Poland's Delivery Deficit is 73%, compared with the survey average of 55%, eleventh out of the eleven countries surveyed.

When it comes to reforms likely to increase the quality of care, giving patients more information about their illness proves to be the most popular. Poles think this will improve things by a sizeable majority of 79% to 16%, equal to France and beaten only by Italy. Some 55–64-year-olds believe this by a larger majority of 81% to 11%, over-65s by a smaller one of 74% to 16%. The majority favouring an increase in the number of medicines and treatments available (70% to 25%) is exceeded only in Britain and Hungary. It is most popular among 35–44-year-olds (by a margin of 74% to 23%) and least popular among the over-65s, who still back it by 62% to 26%. A smaller majority of Poles (53% to 42%) believe increasing the range of doctors and hospitals would improve things. Here the young and the old are the most enthusiastic, 18–24-year-olds back the idea by a majority of 59% to 38% and over-65s do so by 54% to 38%. There is a similar margin in favour of making it easier for patients to spend their own money on healthcare, by 52% to 41%, but here the young and the old diverge. 15–24-year-olds back supplementary spending by 59% to 37%, whereas over-65s oppose the idea by 54% to 34%. Offering patients greater control over public spending on health gains a bare majority of support (by 48% to 46%). Only in Britain and Hungary are people less enthusiastic. Least in favour are the over-65s, who oppose the idea by 50% to 40%.

Poland gives a lower priority to equality of access over the quality of personal care in its health service than any country surveyed other than Britain. Three-quarters (75%) place equality first, against one in five (20%) who do not. Solidarity matters slightly less to men (by a majority of 72% to 23%) than to women who back equality over quality by 77% to 18%. Among age ranges, the over-65s put equality first by 79% to 11% whereas 25–34-year-olds do so only by 71% to 26%. Poland's 'Solidarity Gap' is 55%, lower than the survey average of 62% and ahead only of Britain among the eleven countries studied.

Poles place the greatest store by personal experience when it comes to evaluating sources of health information. They give experience a 'Credibility Gap' rating of +69% (against an average of +63%). Doctors' and nurses' opinions also score highly (Credibility Gap +66% against an average of +74%) though they do so in less overwhelming numbers than any country except Spain and Italy. The media, however, scores more highly as a trustworthy source of information in Poland than in any other country. It has a Credibility Gap of +41%, nearly twice as high as in the next country (France +22%) and

Most reliable sources of health information (Credibility Gap)

	Reliable	*Unreliable*	*Net*
Experience	81	12	69
Doctors/nurses	80	14	66
Media	69	28	41
NGOs	63	22	41
Official statistics	54	40	14
Industry	47	44	3
Politicians	11	87	–76

vastly in excess of the survey average of –4%. NGOs do as well in Poland as elsewhere (Credibility Gap + 41%, survey average +41%) as do official statistics (Credibility Gap +14%, survey average +17%). However, the healthcare industry does slightly worse (Credibility Gap +3%, survey average +16%), as do politicians, distrusted by a majority of 87% to 11% in Poland against an overall average of 78% to 18%.

On taking greater personal responsibility for keeping healthy, 99% of Poles agree they should do this compared with only 1% who don't – the joint highest majority with Hungary. However only 8% of Poles believe that government should play the main role in helping them, the lowest proportion of any country surveyed, while more than three in five (62%) think that doctors should take the lead, the second highest proportion of any country surveyed.

Summary

Poland

Delivery Deficit	73	11th
Solidarity Gap	55	10th
Inferiority Complex	80	1st
Marks out of 10	3.8	11th
Pessimism Ranking	77	2nd
Reform Index	89	2nd

Poland

Commentary

Adam Kruszewski

According to the survey, Poland has the worst healthcare system of those countries which were surveyed, at least as far as the opinion of its own citizens is concerned.

It is worth emphasising, however, that the survey is based on public perceptions and not on outcomes or effects on the health of the population in comparison with investment. But since healthcare is a service industry, the satisfaction of clients, not of healthcare professionals, should, of course, be used to decide its score.

Poland's position at the bottom of the Pessimism Index (eleventh position when performance is measured against aspiration, and also eleventh looking at the health care system as a whole) confirms the very low opinion of Polish citizens towards their healthcare system.

That opinion is influenced by a number of factors. Since the beginning of the 1990s, Poland has undergone a serious and yet rapid transformation. This sort of transformation has been very difficult for some groups, and yet has not appeared to bring with it any immediately positive effects. Especially for frequent users of healthcare, such as older people, those changes have often not been positive at all. Their income is relatively lower than it used to be in comparison with other groups of citizens and they have lost some of the government protection they used to receive under communism. This negative opinion about the general situation in Poland is reflected in the negative opinion of its healthcare system.

Moreover, the comparison between the healthcare system and other parts of the service industry is not positive for the health sector. Since the early 1990s, cinemas, restaurants and shops have all been developing quickly. All these players are operating in a market where the weakest, least preferred by customers – in other words, those that are less client-friendly and more expensive than the competition – go out of business. The inflow of western investors and know-how also helps to improve the sector.

In comparison with the rest of the service industry, the healthcare sector still lags many years behind. The healthcare system is not patient-friendly – it remains bureaucratic, with long waiting times and low-quality healthcare facilities.

As the survey shows, people lack information about their illness and have to rely primarily on their own experience rather than on other trusted sources of information.

This goes some way to explaining why the mass media in Poland score much more highly as a reliable source of health information than in other countries. In recent years, Poland has experienced the advent of an independent media. Journalists now inform the public about many things that were hidden from ordinary people in the past. As a result, people are beginning to believe in what the media tells them, even if the message is often contradictory in different newspapers. But the overall message is similar – all of the press presents a very negative view about the healthcare system in general, and the role of government and politicians in particular.

The government controls the system and seems to believe that only public ownership of providers as well as equality and publicly-run distribution of citizens' healthcare contributions will guarantee protection of the weakest groups in society. They still believe that it is possible to ask people to pay for healthcare proportionally to their income and at the same time to give all citizens the right to use the system according to their needs. The problem is that almost nobody but the government believes that this rule can work.

Therefore Poles believe rather less strongly in equal access than other countries (occupying eleventh position on the Solidarity Gap). Instead, they would prefer a higher quality of personal care. During communism they discovered that equal access is just a slogan which means that access is never equal in a system which assumes it to be so. Instead of true equal access, it simply creates new rules for securing access through personal relationships and informal, cash payments.

Some 95% of hospital beds and over half of outpatient care is still in the hands of the state. In Poland, due to communism, 'public sector' tends to mean ineffective and low quality. Unfortunately, the situation in healthcare confirms this belief. Public facilities are often underfunded, with demotivated staff, long waiting lists and poor customer service.

The National Health Fund is the only payer, and with its

political constraints it has to protect ineffective hospitals, which are often the biggest employers in their area. Poland, with an unemployment rate of almost 20%, has no intention of restructuring hospitals by cutting their headcount. Therefore, newcomers have no opportunity of obtaining contracts from the National Health Fund. Instead, they go to existing, overstaffed facilities with frustrated personnel. Even with those contracts, public providers accumulate debts in the form of overdue liabilities. This makes the situation worse year after year and is borne out by the responses of people surveyed, who believe that healthcare reform is urgently needed. Some 86% said so, putting Poland at the top of the eleven countries surveyed.

Three-quarters of Poles say that healthcare is underfunded, the highest proportion of those surveyed. In Poland, healthcare consumes 6% of GDP, compared with an average of 9% in EU countries. In terms of investment in euros, the comparison is even worse. This inevitably results in lower quality of service, due to low quality of facilities, older and unevenly distributed equipment, and underpaid personnel. Medical staff receive lower salaries than in other countries (not only in western European countries, but also in comparison with the Czech Republic or Hungary) and also lower than it is possible to receive in other professions. This is despite the fact that 70% of expenditure in the healthcare system is attributed to personnel costs.

Low pay results in the frustration of staff, which is then projected on to patients, who are not treated in a patient-friendly environment. Moreover, there is the phenomenon of the so-called 'grey zone', whereby doctors use waiting lists as a tool to obtain additional payments or favours from patients for making access easier. Even if this practice is marginal, it still does not improve the public's overall opinions about the sector.

The Pessimism Ranking and Inferiority Ranking show that Poles believe they have the worst healthcare system among EU countries. However, those scores are subjective, since almost nobody has much experience of using healthcare systems in other countries. What people can use as benchmarks are other parts of the service industry and the private parts of the healthcare system.

While inpatients can only obtain quicker access or better service through informal payments, the outpatient sector is partly privatised. Most services in private health care are still available through direct out-of-pocket payments, but there are also companies offering pre-paid, 'quasi-insurance' services.

Those services operate in opposition to publicly funded, badly managed services with inferior customer service. A few private ambulatory networks are aggressively selling their services to companies as optional extras, beyond the public service outpatient care given to employees as fringe benefits. Currently, additional healthcare benefits have become a standard in big cities, at least among better-paid employees.

The quality of service is measured, access is easy, the level of facilities and equipment is high. The personnel seem to be happy and, due to increased competition in this sector, prices are coming down. Additionally, those services are investment-free to the government and save government money, since services are paid by employers or clients.

Those companies offer a broad ambulatory care service and try to attract the National Health Fund to obtain public contracts. But up until now they have been unsuccessful, since giving away contracts from public providers means an increase in unemployment in the public sector.

A positive benchmark from the private sector and the diminishing position of the public part of the healthcare sector, as well as the conservative attitude of politicians, results in the public's lack of belief in the likely improvement of the situation in the healthcare sector – Poland occupies second position in the Pessimism Ranking. This is especially true since the reform of the healthcare sector in Poland appears to have no positive connotations.

In the last six years, Poland has undergone a constant process of reform. The first reform took place in 1999, splitting the function of payer and provider. It created national compulsory healthcare insurance, financed through wage deductions. These deductions flow to seventeen public sick funds. Sick funds then contract for healthcare services with public and private sector providers. The reforms had a major impact on the behaviour of providers: public sector providers started facing market disciplines, and private sector providers were given the opportunity to compete with the public sector.

But after a year or two of optimism, the National Health Fund realised that it was under major pressure from local governments, responsible for badly managed providers with growing sums of unpaid liabilities. On the other hand, politicians felt there was a lack of control over the billions of euros paid through contracts to the sector. Regional Sickness Funds were therefore reunited in 1992, becoming subsidiaries of the central National Health Fund.

In 2003, the mass media and experts once again started a

debate about the launch of private healthcare insurance. At the request of the Minister of Economy, a group of experts prepared a project showing ways of introducing private healthcare insurance. The project was presented to the government at the beginning of 2004. Since then, there has been serious discussion about the role of the private sector in general and private healthcare insurance in particular in the sector.

Given the worsening cash flow situation in hospitals, and the increasing public demand for improvements in the situation, the government's only chance will be to invite private capital to invest in the sector, as well as allowing private individuals to buy better services officially instead of obtaining them unofficially.

Currently the Parliament is voting to repay part of the debts of public hospitals yet again. Politicians still seem to believe that this financial relief will help hospitals to restructure themselves. A more likely scenario is that this will not change the situation. Sooner rather than later, politicians will have no choice but to let private companies invest in the healthcare sector, bringing with them increased efficiency and increases in patient satisfaction.

Slovakia

Slovakia

Poll and analysis

Rick Nye

Context

Most important features of healthcare and health system's ability to deliver them

	Important	*Good*	*Net*
The time between diagnosis and treatment	96	15	81
Being treated at a time and a place to suit you	95	24	71
Having enough information to make an informed choice about your treatment	95	24	71
Being treated using the latest medicines/technology	94	24	70
Being treated by a doctor of your choice	89	49	40
Average delivery deficit			**67**

Which is more important to you about your health system?
(Solidarity Gap)

	Equality of access	*Quality of personal care*	*Net*
Hungary	88	11	77
Netherlands	84	15	69
Italy	84	15	69
Spain	83	17	66
Sweden	81	17	64
Germany	81	18	63
Czech Republic	81	18	63
Average	**80**	**18**	**62**
Slovakia	80	18	62
France	78	21	57
Poland	75	20	55
Britain	69	31	38

How do other European health systems perform compared with your own? (Inferiority Complex)

	Better	*The same*	*Worse*	*Better minus the same/worse*
Poland	90	4	5	80
Hungary	78	14	9	55
Slovakia	73	12	15	46
Czech Republic	65	26	10	28
Italy	63	26	11	26
Britain	60	29	12	19
Average	**54**	**26**	**20**	**8**
Spain	42	35	26	–19
Germany	38	27	35	–24
Netherlands	34	41	25	–32
Sweden	24	43	34	–53
France	20	31	48	–59

Health System: marks out of 10

France	6.9	**Average**	**5.6**
Netherlands	6.7	Czech Republic	5.3
Spain	6.7	Germany	5.1
Britain	5.9	Hungary	5.1
Sweden	5.8	Slovakia	4.4
Italy	5.8	Poland	3.8

Prospects for healthcare in 10 years' time if your system remains unreformed (Pessimism Ranking)

	Improve	*Stay the same*	*Get worse*	*Stay the same/get worse minus improve*
Germany	4	12	80	88
Poland	10	13	74	77
Sweden	11	18	68	75
Netherlands	14	20	64	70
Spain	14	22	58	66
Average	**16**	**20**	**60**	**65**
Britain	17	22	60	65
France	17	21	59	63
Czech Republic	16	25	54	63
Slovakia	21	17	56	52
Italy	21	31	40	50
Hungary	27	19	50	42

Does your health system need reforming? (Reform Index)

	Yes (urgently)	*Yes*	*No*	*Yes (urgently)/yes minus no*
Hungary	85	10	2	93
Poland	86	7	4	89
Germany	76	14	7	83
Czech Republic	64	22	6	80
Slovakia	62	22	6	78
Britain	63	24	10	77
Average	**65**	**21**	**9**	**77**
France	65	20	11	74
Italy	60	24	10	74
Sweden	58	24	11	71
Spain	46	35	14	67
Netherlands	54	24	15	63

Analysis

On the overall measure of delivery against aspirations for healthcare, Slovakia ranks its system among the worst of any country surveyed, above only Poland. Perhaps because of this, more people in Slovakia believe their healthcare system to be underfunded than in any other country. Slovaks also believe in larger numbers than in any other country except Poland and Hungary that other nations' healthcare systems are better than theirs. However, the number of Slovaks who think that extra money for health should come from higher personal taxation is smaller than in any other nation except Hungary. It is unsurprising, particularly given the proximity of the Czech Republic, that Slovaks are more willing to travel abroad for treatment than people in any other country surveyed. Slovaks rate their health system 4.4 out of 10, the second lowest mark of the eleven EU countries surveyed.

Over half of Slovaks (56%) believe healthcare will get worse without reform over the next decade. More than three-fifths (62%) of those aged 35–44 believe this, compared with just under a half (46%) of over-65s. Around one in six Slovaks (17%) believe standards will remain the same, and one in five (21%) think things will improve in the absence of reform. This gives Slovakia a 'Pessimism Ranking' of 52%, below the survey average of 65% and ahead only of Italy and Hungary.

When it comes to the need for reform, more than three in five Slovaks (62%) think this is urgent, including more than two-thirds (68%) of 25-34-year-olds and 66% of 35-44-year-olds. A further fifth (22%) think reform is desirable, while only 6% say reform is unnecessary, including 9% of those aged over 65. Slovakia's 'Reform Index' score is therefore 78%, fractionally above the survey average of 77% putting it behind the Czech Republic, Germany, Poland and Hungary in the survey.

More Slovaks feel that their healthcare system is underfunded than in any other country. More than three-quarters (76%) believe this, including 81% of 15–24-year-olds and 83% of 25–34-year-olds. Only one in six Slovaks (15%) think their healthcare system has the about the right amount of money, and just 4% think it has too much. Relative to other European countries, 80% of Slovaks who express an opinion think that other nations have more money to spend on health. Just 8% think other countries spend about the same amount of money on health, and 12% think they spend less.

Nevertheless, only 10% of Slovaks think that extra money for healthcare should come from higher personal taxes, the second lowest total after Hungary. This includes 15% of 15–24-year-olds, but only 7% of 55–64-year-olds. More than half (51%) of Slovaks would like to see the extra money come from higher costs on business, again the highest proportion of any country surveyed.

When it comes to comparative performance, three-quarters (73%) of those Slovaks expressing an opinion believe other countries' healthcare systems perform better, 12% think they perform similarly and 15% think they perform more poorly. This gives Slovakia an 'Inferiority Complex' score of 46%, beaten only by Poland and Hungary.

The priorities of Slovaks when it comes to the measures used to derive the 'Delivery Deficit' are broadly similar to those of the other countries surveyed. Slightly more people in Slovakia value being treated at a time and place to suit them (95% against a survey average of 91%) and being treated by a doctor of their choice (89% against an average of 86%). But the biggest difference is in the number rating the use of latest medicines and technology as important: 94% against an average of 88%. In terms of delivery, Slovakia performs below the average on every measure. This is most striking on the time taken between diagnosis and treatment, where fewer than one in six (15%) give the Slovak system a rating of 'good', and on access to the latest medicines and technology, where fewer than a quarter (24%) say their system is good. Slovakia's overall Delivery Deficit is 67%, second to last, and ahead of only Poland.

It is perhaps unsurprising then that Slovaks express the greatest willingness to travel abroad for treatment of any country so far surveyed. Nearly four-fifths (79%) say they are prepared to do this, including 89% of 15–24-year-olds. Even a majority of those aged 65 and over say they would be willing to travel for treatment if their healthcare system paid for it, by 53% to 44%.

Slovaks believe that giving patients more information about their illnesses is more likely to increase standards of care than any other reform they were asked to comment on. More than two-thirds (70%) believe this, including three-quarters (75%) of 15–44-year-olds, but only 60% of those aged 55 and over. Over two-thirds believe increasing the number of medicines and treatments would help, including three-quarters (74%) of 15–44-year-olds. A clear majority, by 58% to 35%, also believe that giving patients more control over public spending on health would improve healthcare quality. Slightly less than half of Slovaks (49%) believe extending the range of doctors and hospitals is likely to lead to greater quality, but this is still slightly larger than the 45% who do not. The country is more evenly divided about the effect of making it easier for patients to supplement health spending from their own income. 47% believe this would help, against 45% who do not. Men who back the idea by 51% to 44% are slightly keener than women, who marginally oppose it by 45% to 46%. 15–44-year-olds are clearly in favour (by 58% to 39%), but the over-55s are against by 55% to 31%.

By a wide margin, Slovaks think offering everyone equal access to the same standards of healthcare is more important to their health system than offering access to the best possible care for themselves and their family. Four out of five (80%) say equality comes first, compared with 18% who stress quality

Reforms most likely to increase the quality of care

	Likely	*Not likely*	*Net*
Giving patients more information about their illness	70	25	45
Increasing number of medicines and treatments	67	26	41
Giving patients more control over public spending on health	58	35	23
Increasing range of doctors and hospitals	49	45	4
Making it easier for patients to spend their own money on health	47	45	2

of personal care. There is a slight difference between the sexes here. For males, 77% think equality is more important, whereas 81% of women believe the same. There is a bigger difference between 35–44-year-olds, who back equality over quality by 71% to 26%, and those aged 65 and over, who do so by 88% to 10%. Slovakia's overall 'Solidarity Gap' rating is 62%, in line with the survey average.

On the whole, Slovaks are slightly less sceptical than average when it comes to evaluating the trustworthiness of sources of information about healthcare. Their most trusted source is the opinions of doctors or nurses. More than four out of five (85%) Slovaks believe them to be reliable, against 10% who do not. This Credibility Gap of +75% is line with the survey average of +74%.

Slovaks rate personal experience and the experience of friends and family as highly as other countries. 79% find them reliable, against 17% who find them unreliable (Credibility Gap +62%, against an average of 63%). Slovakia also shares a general

Most reliable sources of health information (Credibility Gap)

	Reliable	*Unreliable*	*Net*
Doctors/nurses	85	10	75
Experience	79	17	62
NGOs	59	25	34
Industry	63	30	33
Official statistics	63	33	30
Media	48	48	0
Politicians	22	75	–53

scepticism about politicians' statements by 22% to 75%, but this drops to 17% against 78% among the over-65s. Overall, politicians enjoy a Credibility Gap of –53% in Slovakia, against the survey average of –60%. Slovakia is however kinder to the media. Some 48% find media stories reliable – as many as do not. There is a slight gender gap here, with men believing the media by 52% to 45% and women taking the opposite view. This makes Slovakia only one of three countries (France and Poland being the other two) where a majority are not sceptical.

Slovaks are also more likely to believe official statistics (by 63% to 33%) than most other countries, and the Credibility Gap here is +17% rather than +30%, though older Slovaks are more sceptical – 55–64-year-olds believe them by 56% to 40% and the over-65s by 54% to 37%. Industry sources also fare better. They are believed by 63% to 30% (Credibility Gap +33%, compared with an average of +16%). There is again a difference in gender here, with women more likely to believe industry information by 67% to 26%, whereas men do so by 59% to 35%.

Non-governmental organisations fare slightly worse, however. Though believed on balance by 59% of Slovaks against 25%, among over-65s this drops to 43% against 29%, and their overall Credibility Gap of +34% is worse only in Sweden and the Czech Republic, and is below the survey average of +41%.

Slovaks agree by a wide margin that they should take more responsibility for keeping themselves healthy, by 96% to 2%. Nearly a half (46%) believe that doctors have the greatest role in helping them compared with a third (31%) who think that government should take the lead. More men (36%) think this than women (26%). Meanwhile, 11% say that other health professionals should take the lead, the highest proportion in any country surveyed except for Britain and Sweden.

Summary

Slovakia

Delivery Deficit	67	10th
Solidarity Gap	62	8th
Inferiority Complex	46	3rd
Marks out of 10	4.4	10th
Pessimism Ranking	52	9th
Reform Index	78	5th

Slovakia

Commentary

Henrieta Madarová and Martin Stefunko

The issue of healthcare reform is not new in Slovakia. The term has been mentioned more often than ever before by politicians, the media and health professionals since the last election in 2002. In October 2002, the new minister of health, Rudolf Zajac, launched a challenging, complex and far-reaching healthcare reform.

According to Mr Zajac and his principal adviser, economist Peter Pazitny, the main problems of the existing healthcare system were as follows:[1]

- Insufficient and unequal access to healthcare services exacerbated by corruption.
- Allocative and technical inefficiency in healthcare provision. The healthcare market is characterised by a surplus of low-quality facilities, and there are no mechanisms in place to push low-quality and inefficient providers out of the market.
- Soft budget constraints of healthcare providers and health

insurance companies resulting in high indebtness of the mainly public healthcare sector to overwhelmingly private suppliers.

- Low quality of healthcare provided due to absence of competition between healthcare providers and health insurance companies.
- No definition of the scope of healthcare services eligible under the public health insurance scheme and, as a consequence, little scope for private health insurance and co-payments. The healthcare system is financially unbalanced due to the boundless scope of healthcare services and the improper structure of healthcare spending – much money and emphasis is put on in-patient care rather than on prevention and out-patient treatment.
- Changing structure of diseases[2] – from communicable to non-communicable diseases (e.g. 52.5% of deaths are due to cardiovascular diseases and 22.8% due to oncological diseases).

The current government's healthcare reform has been designed and is being implemented in two steps. The first step is a series of stabilisation measures focused on curbing the growth of debts in the healthcare sector and restricting excessive consumption of healthcare services. These came into force on 1 July 2003 and include:

1 Separating healthcare services from services connected to the provision of healthcare – e.g. non-urgent ambulance transportation to and from a healthcare facility, in-patient facility accommodation, in-patient facility boarding.

2 Introduction of co-payments:

- 20 SKK per out-patient and first-aid visit (with a number of exceptions – e.g. people from lower socio-economic groups, children, chronically ill patients, etc.)
- 20 SKK per medicine prescription (the same as above mentioned, including disabled people)
- 50 SKK per bed-day in in-patient facility (up to 21 days only)
- 2 SKK per km of non-urgent ambulance transportation

3 New measures in drug policy:

- Grouping drugs by a new method through active substances in 122 anatomical-therapeutical classes
- New and more transparent rules for the categorisation of drugs into three different co-payment categories (the first category of drugs with no co-payment, the second with partial co-payment, and the third with full co-payment). This is being done more frequently by means of two rounds of public bidding
- Introduction of a so-called 'fixed co-payment', which means a fixed percentage share of the co-payment by patients of the total price of a drug

The introduction of the above-mentioned stabilisation measures decreased the number of visits to primary care doctors by 10% during the second half of 2003 and the number of the visits to first-aid doctors by 13%. At the same time, the dynamic of growth of health insurance companies' spending improved dramatically (see Figure 7).

The second stage of reform concerned so-called 'system

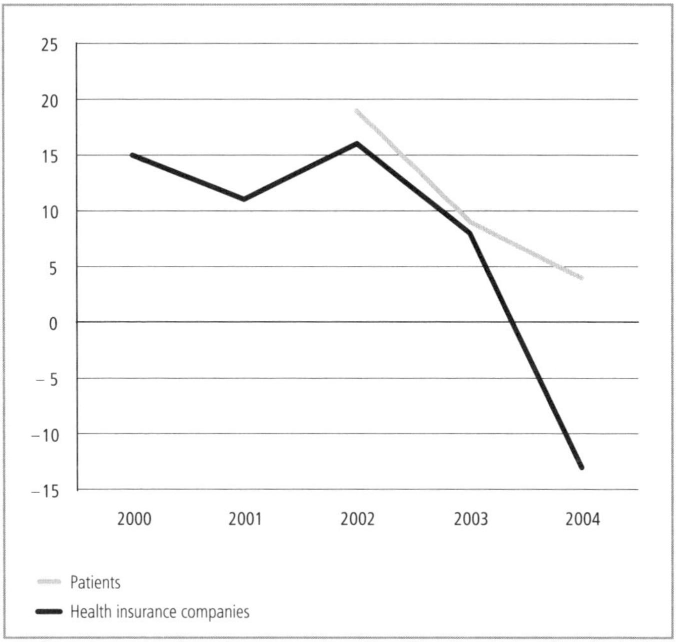

Figure 7 **Dynamic of drug spending — HIC and patients**

measures'. These consisted of six new laws defining the new, more market-oriented legislative framework for players in the health sector (e.g. health insurance companies and their shareholders, hospitals and their owners, out-patient doctors, and pharmacies and their owners). The new laws are as follows:

- Act on Health Insurance
- Act on Health Insurance Companies and Healthcare Surveillance Authority
- Act on Healthcare

- Act on the Scope of Healthcare Services Covered by the Public Health Insurance Scheme
- Act on Healthcare Emergency Service
- Act on Healthcare Providers

These laws were approved by the Parliament in the autumn of 2004 and have been effective since 1 January 2005. The main goals of the new healthcare reform legislation are:

- Creation of a self-regulatory environment and incentives for patients to take care and improve their health status (health is seen as an individual not a public good)
- Equal treatment for equal need – the scope of services covered by the public health insurance scheme is defined, as is the process of setting the legal co-payments for patients, thus leaving space for individual health insurance
- Guarantee of protection against individual catastrophic-cost scenarios, while increasing financial self-responsibility with respect to vulnerable groups (e.g. chronically ill patients, children)
- Increase in allocative efficiency of health insurance companies, and introduction of management of patients and selective contracting with healthcare providers
- Introduction of hard budget constraints and competition among healthcare providers and health insurance companies (free entry to highly regulated market, reduction of the role and monopolistic power of medical chambers)
- Improvement of the quality of healthcare provided and greater dissemination of information about it

At the moment, the process of implementation of the new legislation is on hold, so it is not possible yet to derive any conclusions from it or to discuss the results objectively.

As far as public opinion goes, at the time when the poll was conducted, the above-described healthcare reform had already been approved in Parliament in spite of strong disagreement by the opposition, health professionals and a number of health professional associations. The opinion of citizens and patients was not officially presented in the Parliamentary discussions, because these groups are highly fragmented. But according to an opinion poll conducted by the agency Focus[3] in December 2002 and January 2004, the status of the healthcare sector was perceived as the third most serious problem (40% and 37% respectively) after decreasing living standards and unemployment.

In spite of the poor perception of the performance of the Slovak healthcare system (Slovaks rate their system at 4.4 out of 10, according to the poll outcomes), Slovaks' eagerness for healthcare reform is, nevertheless, rated as the lowest among the new member countries (84% said that healthcare reform is needed or is needed urgently). This might be due to the number of other reforms that have been launched at the same time (including tax reform, social security system reform and pension scheme reform) and their rather negative impact on the living standard of Slovaks in the short term. Healthcare reform steps (mainly various types of co-payments) implemented until that time had also been viewed as having a negative impact on citizens' material wellbeing, although the Focus poll showed that only approximately 2% of people were discouraged from making a medical visit or taking out a drug prescription as a result of these new co-payments.

Slovakia, along with all other new EU member states, paradoxically perceives a higher need for reform than other surveyed 'old EU-member countries', but, on the other hand, is also less pessimistic about the prospects if no reform takes place.

According to the poll, more Slovaks feel that their healthcare system is underfunded than in any other country. This might be due to the arguments of Slovakia's Parliamentary opposition against healthcare reform. In their opinion, the main problem of the Slovak healthcare sector lies in the lack of funds and not in the system *per se*. Their proposals for healthcare reform are mainly focused on increasing the amount of money in the healthcare sector without any institutional change. The main argument is that the subsidised rate paid by the state (i.e. by the Ministry of Finance) for the 'state' insurees (children, the unemployed, pensioners, etc.) is not high enough (486 SKK as compared to approximately 2,010 SKK per average employee). Of course, in the end all the public money in the health sector comes from citizens anyway, either through taxes or premiums.

Connected to this, a very interesting outcome of the results is the data about the most important means for improving the quality of healthcare. Only 47% of the Slovak population think that the quality of healthcare services can be enhanced by patients' ability to spend additional money from their own pockets. The age distribution of the results is in line with the perception of the elderly that they have been paying contributions to the healthcare system throughout their lives and, as a result, they now feel they should have the right to unlimited free healthcare. This view is also supported by the ambiguous Article 40 in the Slovakian Constitution, which states that 'Everybody has the right to free healthcare under the conditions stated by the law.' It also explains another result of the poll – that equal access to the same standards of healthcare for everyone is seen as being a more important value than offering access to the best possible care for individuals and their families.

Although 96% of respondents admit they should take more responsibility for keeping themselves healthy, only 47% (see above) are ready to pay more themselves for their consumption of healthcare services, and 58% would like to take more control over public spending on healthcare. On the other hand, 58% of the population would prefer to close the perceived healthcare sector funding gap by imposing higher costs on business. This indicates that the willingness to take more individual responsibility for health is nominal rather than real.

Another finding from the poll is that Slovaks perceive a significant lack of information about the healthcare system, their health status and possible treatments. At the moment there is no services evaluation system in place for monitoring the quality of healthcare, and no institution or formal system protecting patients' rights and safety or controlling doctors and the type and quality of healthcare provided.

One very interesting finding is the perception of the surveyed group that there is no lack of medical and hospital capacity, despite low satisfaction with patients' ability to get treatment at a place and time to suit them and also with the time span between diagnosis and subsequent treatment. This underlines the behaviour of healthcare sector players that evolved in the public system, where there was a lack of competition and a high degree of government regulation. Healthcare providers became used to making their services artificially inaccessible or scarce for patients. Instead, they focused their attention on rent-seeking (informal payments from patients for providing artificially scarce treatment, and from suppliers for paying for supplied goods on time) and on negotiation with health insurance companies about the contracted volume of provided healthcare. Patients and their treatment came a poor second.

For example, due to decreased volumes being contracted, out-patient doctors simply shorten their working hours or take holidays more often because they usually fulfil the amount of services contracted for them by the 20th of the month. This might seem like an argument for underfunding the system, but we should keep in mind that Slovakia inherited a highly institutionalised system from the communist regime, with nearly 150 in-patient facilities all around the country.

We might instead draw the conclusion that in Slovakia the problem is not the shortage of available healthcare sector funds and capacity, but rather the lack of effective allocation of these funds and utilisation of capacity. Thus we should focus our efforts on the reduction of bad management caused by too much state regulation and too few market drivers, and on the introduction of incentives for private ownership, profit-seeking, entrepreneurship and innovation.

Notes

1 Peter Pazitny and Rudolf Zajac: *Strategia reformy zdravotnictva – realnej reformy pre obcana* (*Health care reform strategy – real reform for the citizen*), M.E.S.A.10 2001

2 Concept for the provision of healthcare in the Slovak republic, Ministry of Health, approved by the Cabinet of the Slovak Republic

3 *Postoje verejnosti k otázke reformy zdravotníctva (Attitudes of citizens towards the health sector reform)*, Focus, January 2004

Appendix

Poll structure and statistics

- The three countries surveyed were Hungary, Poland and Slovakia.
- 3,000 interviews were conducted over the phone between 17 January and 7 February 2005.
- For each country, 1,000 interviews were conducted among a sample aged 15+ representative of the age, gender and regional composition of the country.
- Data from each 1,000-person sample is accurate to within ± 3%.
- Each survey has a confidence level of 95%, i.e. if the same poll were repeated among other random samples it would yield the same results within the margin of error described above on 19 out of 20 occasions.

Tot/Ans = Total number of answers received
%/Ans = Percentage of those answering
%/Resp = Percentage of respondents (i.e. those completing the survey)

Final top-line findings

Q1a. When was the last time you personally used one of the following healthcare services?

A family doctor or GP service?

	Tot/Ans	*%/Ans*	*%/Resp*
1. In the last week	566	18.8	18.8
2. In the last month	737	24.5	24.5
3. In the last 3 months	447	14.9	14.9
4. In the last year	632	21.0	21.0
5. More than a year ago	561	18.7	18.7
6. Never	63	2.1	2.1

Q1b. When was the last time you personally used one of the following healthcare services?

A hospital doctor?

	Tot/Ans	*%/Ans*	*%/Resp*
1. In the last week	162	5.4	5.4
2. In the last month	222	7.4	7.4
3. In the last 3 months	215	7.2	7.2
4. In the last year	528	17.6	17.6
5. More than a year ago	1,571	52.3	52.3
6. Never	308	10.2	10.2

Q2. Thinking about the general state of [country X's] healthcare system today, how would you rate its performance between 0 and 10, where 0 means it is performing extremely badly and 10 means its performance is outstanding?

0 min, 10 max, 6.02 mean

	Tot/Ans	*%/Ans*	*%/Resp*
Don't know	92	3.1	3.1

Q3. How good would you say [country X's] healthcare system is at meeting the individual needs of the patients it treats?

	Tot/Ans	*%/Ans*	*%/Resp*
1. Very good	44	1.5	1.5
2. Good	422	14.0	14.0
3. Fair	1,159	38.6	38.6
4. Poor	965	32.1	32.1
5. Very poor	324	10.8	10.8
6. Don't know	92	3.1	3.1

Q4. Now thinking about other healthcare systems in Europe, how well do you think they perform on average compared to [country X's]?

	Tot/Ans	*%/Ans*	*%/Resp*
1. Much better	880	29.3	29.3
2. Slightly better	814	27.1	27.1
3. About the same	211	7.0	7.0
4. Slightly worse	134	4.5	4.5
5. Much worse	69	2.3	2.3
6. Don't know	898	29.9	29.9

Q5. Thinking about the level of funding of [country X's] healthcare system/health service today, would you say it has:

	Tot/Ans	*%/Ans*	*%/Resp*
1. Significantly too little money	1,346	44.8	44.8
2. Slightly too little money	906	30.1	30.1
3. About the right amount of money	421	14.0	14.0
4. Slightly too much money	87	2.9	2.9
5. Significantly too much money	59	2.0	2.0
6. Don't know	187	6.2	6.2

Q6. Now thinking about other healthcare systems in Europe, how much money would you say they have spent on them compared to [country X's]?

	Tot/Ans	*%/Ans*	*%/Resp*
1. A lot more money	1,343	44.7	44.7
2. Slightly more money	580	19.3	19.3
3. About the same amount of money	136	4.5	4.5
4. Slightly less money	133	4.4	4.4
5. A lot less money	119	4.0	4.0
6. Don't know	695	23.1	23.1

Q7. Would you personally be prepared to travel to another European country for an operation if your own healthcare system paid for it?

	Tot/Ans	*%/Ans*	*%/Resp*
1. Yes	2,136	71.1	71.1
2. No	758	25.2	25.2
3. Don't know	112	3.7	3.7

Q8. Which of these statements comes closest to your view of how [country X's] healthcare system works today?

	Tot/Ans	*%/Ans*	*%/Resp*
1. It does not offer access to care for everyone	822	27.3	27.3
2. It offers access to care for everyone, but individual patients do not always receive the best treatment available when they need it	1,717	57.1	57.1
3. It offers the best treatment available to every patient when they need it	393	13.1	13.1
4. Don't know	74	2.5	2.5

Q9. Which of these is more important to you personally when it comes to [country X's] healthcare system?

	Tot/Ans	*%/Ans*	*%/Resp*
1. Giving everyone equal access to the same standards of care	2,422	80.6	80.6
2. Ensuring that you and your family have access to the best possible care	493	16.4	16.4
Don't know	91	3.0	3.0

Q10. If the way [country X's] current healthcare system is run remains unchanged for the next ten years, what will happen to the quality of care in [country X]?

	Tot/Ans	*%/Ans*	*%/Resp*
1. It will improve a lot	86	2.9	2.9
2. It will improve a little	500	16.6	16.6
3. It will stay about the same	485	16.1	16.1
4. It will worsen a little	642	21.4	21.4
5. It will worsen a lot	1,158	38.5	38.5
6. Don't know	135	4.5	4.5

Q11. Does the way healthcare is organised in [country X] need reform?

	Tot/Ans	*%/Ans*	*%/Resp*
1. Yes – urgently	2,330	77.5	77.5
2. Yes – but not really urgent	389	12.9	12.9
3. No	122	4.1	4.1
4. Don't know	165	5.5	5.5

Q12. I am going to read out a list of sources for information about how well [country X's] healthcare system is performing. In each case can you tell me how reliable you think they are?

Official statistics?

	Tot/Ans	*%/Ans*	*%/Resp*
1. Very reliable	127	4.2	4.2
2. Somewhat reliable	1,605	53.4	53.4
3. Not very reliable	832	27.7	27.7
4. Not at all reliable	283	9.4	9.4
5. Don't know	159	5.3	5.3

Politicians' statements?

	Tot/Ans	*%/Ans*	*%/Resp*
1. Very reliable	23	0.8	0.8
2. Somewhat reliable	573	19.1	19.1
3. Not very reliable	1,125	37.4	37.4
4. Not at all reliable	1,181	39.3	39.3
5. Don't know	104	3.5	3.5

Stories in the media?

	Tot/Ans	*%/Ans*	*%/Resp*
1. Very reliable	128	4.3	4.3
2. Somewhat reliable	1,521	50.6	50.6
3. Not very reliable	937	31.2	31.2
4. Not at all reliable	324	10.8	10.8
5. Don't know	96	3.2	3.2

Opinions of doctors and nurses?

	Tot/Ans	*%/Ans*	*%/Resp*
1. Very reliable	855	28.4	28.4
2. Somewhat reliable	1,667	55.5	55.5
3. Not very reliable	275	9.1	9.1
4. Not at all reliable	49	1.6	1.6
5. Don't know	160	5.3	5.3

Information from the healthcare industry (e.g. insurers or pharmaceutical companies)?

	Tot/Ans	*%/Ans*	*%/Resp*
1. Very reliable	215	7.2	7.2
2. Somewhat reliable	1,385	46.1	46.1
3. Not very reliable	850	28.3	28.3
4. Not at all reliable	267	8.9	8.9
5. Don't know	289	9.6	9.6

Information from NGOs (e.g. patients' advocates and pressure groups)?

	Tot/Ans	*%/Ans*	*%/Resp*
1. Very reliable	335	11.1	11.1
2. Somewhat reliable	1,471	48.9	48.9
3. Not very reliable	509	16.9	16.9
4. Not at all reliable	150	5.0	5.0
5. Don't know	541	18.0	18.0

Personal experience/experience of friends and relatives?

	Tot/Ans	*%/Ans*	*%/Resp*
1. Very reliable	1,145	38.1	38.1
2. Somewhat reliable	1,329	44.2	44.2
3. Not very reliable	315	10.5	10.5
4. Not at all reliable	73	2.4	2.4
5. Don't know	144	4.8	4.8

Q13a. I am going to read a list of factors associated with good-quality healthcare. For each one, can you tell me how important they are to you personally?

The time between diagnosis and treatment?

	Tot/Ans	*%/Ans*	*%/Resp*
1. Very important	2,660	88.5	88.5
2. Somewhat important	261	8.7	8.7
3. Not very important	31	1.0	1.0
4. Not at all important	10	0.3	0.3
5. Don't know	44	1.5	1.5

Being treated at a time and a place to suit you?

	Tot/Ans	*%/Ans*	*%/Resp*
1. Very important	2,451	81.5	81.5
2. Somewhat important	449	14.9	14.9
3. Not very important	69	2.3	2.3
4. Not at all important	14	0.5	0.5
5. Don't know	23	0.8	0.8

Being treated by the doctor of your choice?

	Tot/Ans	*%/Ans*	*%/Resp*
1. Very important	2,069	68.8	68.8
2. Somewhat important	688	22.9	22.9
3. Not very important	191	6.4	6.4
4. Not at all important	32	1.1	1.1
5. Don't know	26	0.9	0.9

Being treated using the latest medicines or technology?

	Tot/Ans	*%/Ans*	*%/Resp*
1. Very important	1,997	66.4	66.4
2. Somewhat important	721	24.0	24.0
3. Not very important	190	6.3	6.3
4. Not at all important	28	0.9	0.9
5. Don't know	70	2.3	2.3

Having enough information to make an informed choice about your treatment?

	Tot/Ans	*%/Ans*	*%/Resp*
1. Very important	2,518	83.8	83.8
2. Somewhat important	371	12.3	12.3
3. Not very important	57	1.9	1.9
4. Not at all important	10	0.3	0.3
5. Don't know	50	1.7	1.7

Q13b. I am going to read a list of factors associated with good-quality healthcare. For each one, can you tell me how well do you think [country X's] health system is currently performing in ...?

The time between diagnosis and treatment?

	Tot/Ans	*%/Ans*	*%/Resp*
1. Good	468	15.6	15.6
2. Fair	1,292	43.0	43.0
3. Poor	1,102	36.7	36.7
4. Don't know	144	4.8	4.8

Being treated at a time and a place to suit you?

	Tot/Ans	*%/Ans*	*%/Resp*
1. Good	723	24.1	24.1
2. Fair	1,294	43.0	43.0
3. Poor	866	28.8	28.8
4. Don't know	123	4.1	4.1

Being treated by the doctor of your choice?

	Tot/Ans	*%/Ans*	*%/Resp*
1. Good	1,470	48.9	48.9
2. Fair	968	32.2	32.2
3. Poor	443	14.7	14.7
4. Don't know	125	4.2	4.2

Being treated using the latest medicines or technology?

	Tot/Ans	*%/Ans*	*%/Resp*
1. Good	764	25.4	25.4
2. Fair	1,045	34.8	34.8
3. Poor	887	29.5	29.5
4. Don't know	310	10.3	10.3

Having enough information to make an informed choice about your treatment?

	Tot/Ans	*%/Ans*	*%/Resp*
1. Good	870	28.9	28.9
2. Fair	1,134	37.7	37.7
3. Poor	850	28.3	28.3
4. Don't know	152	5.1	5.1

Q14. I am going to read out a list of possible reforms to healthcare in [country X]. For each one, can you tell me how likely they are to increase the quality of care in your country?

Increasing the range of doctors and hospitals where you can choose to be treated?

	Tot/Ans	*%/Ans*	*%/Resp*
1. Very likely	638	21.2	21.2
2. Quite likely	1,037	34.5	34.5
3. Not very likely	947	31.5	31.5
4. Not at all likely	234	7.8	7.8
5. Don't know	150	5.0	5.0

Increasing the number of medicines or treatments that you or your doctor can choose from?

	Tot/Ans	*%/Ans*	*%/Resp*
1. Very likely	831	27.6	27.6
2. Quite likely	1,335	44.4	44.4
3. Not very likely	570	19.0	19.0
4. Not at all likely	100	3.3	3.3
5. Don't know	170	5.7	5.7

Giving patients more control over the way public funds on health are spent?

	Tot/Ans	*%/Ans*	*%/Resp*
1. Very likely	664	22.1	22.1
2. Quite likely	774	25.7	25.7
3. Not very likely	921	30.6	30.6
4. Not at all likely	441	14.7	14.7
5. Don't know	206	6.9	6.9

Making it easier for patients to supplement current spending on health with their own money?

	Tot/Ans	*%/Ans*	*%/Resp*
1. Very likely	582	19.4	19.4
2. Quite likely	948	31.5	31.5
3. Not very likely	846	28.1	28.1
4. Not at all likely	380	12.6	12.6
5. Don't know	250	8.3	8.3

Giving patients more information about their illness so they can exercise more choice in how they are treated?

	Tot/Ans	*%/Ans*	*%/Resp*
1. Very likely	1,038	34.5	34.5
2. Quite likely	1,081	36.0	36.0
3. Not very likely	587	19.5	19.5
4. Not at all likely	167	5.6	5.6
5. Don't know	133	4.4	4.4

Q15. Given the pressures of an ageing population, advances in medical science and competing priorities for social spending, do you think that people should take greater responsibility for keeping themselves healthy?

	Tot/Ans	*%/Ans*	*%/Resp*
1. Yes	2,941	97.8	97.8
2. No	37	1.2	1.2
3. Don't know	28	0.9	0.9

Q16a. And who do you think has the greatest role to play in helping people keep themselves healthy?

	Tot/Ans	*%/Ans*	*%/Resp*
1. Governments	833	27.7	27.7
2. Doctors	1,363	45.3	45.3
3. Pharmaceutical companies	64	2.1	2.1
4. Other health professionals (e.g. pharmacists, public health workers, nurses)	289	9.6	9.6
5. Non-profit groups	173	5.8	5.8
6. Don't know	284	9.4	9.4

Q16b. Could you please name two others who have a role to play (in helping people keep themselves healthy)?

	Tot/Ans	*%/Ans*	*%/Resp*
1. Governments	635	23.3	21.1
2. Doctors	964	35.4	32.1
3. Pharmaceutical companies	729	26.8	24.3
4. Other health professionals (e.g. pharmacists, public health workers, nurses)	1,242	45.6	41.3
5. Non-profit groups	592	21.7	19.7
6. Don't know	202	7.4	6.7
7. No answer	156	5.7	5.2

Q17a. Given the pressures I just mentioned on healthcare provision in the future, more spending is likely to be needed on health. Where do you think most of this extra money should come from?

	Tot/Ans	*%/Ans*	*%/Resp*
1. Higher taxes on individuals	327	10.9	10.9
2. More personal spending by individuals	422	14.0	14.0
3. Higher taxes or employment costs paid by businesses	1,324	44.0	44.0
4. Don't know	933	31.0	31.0

Q17b. And where do you think most of this money will end up coming from?

	Tot/Ans	*%/Ans*	*%/Resp*
1. Higher taxes on individuals	1,009	33.6	33.6
2. More personal spending by individuals	682	22.7	22.7
3. Higher taxes or employment costs paid by businesses	670	22.3	22.3
4. Don't know	645	21.5	21.5